POWER SELLING
CONSULT & COLLABORATE TO
GAIN COMPETITIVE DISTINCTION

STEVEN POWER

Ventura, California

**PowerSelling: Consult and Collaborate
to Gain Competitive Distinction
© 2004 by Power2Be Media**

Book design by Sara Patton
Manufactured in the United States of America

ISBN 0-9746562-0-8

2975 Seahorse Avenue
Ventura, CA 93001

Contents

Acknowledgments

First, there is Mike Riordan of Riordan and Associates, who, if not for his mentorship, helpfulness, and support in referring clients early in my consulting career, Sales & Marketing Solutions International would not have made it past the first year. Mike has taught me to understand that *process* is the key to transferring attitudes, skills, and knowledge so ordinary people can achieve extraordinary results. He has also taught me never to forget the importance of the "human connection" in sales, business and life.

Next, my clients, some of whom took risk early on in embracing me as their consultant and testing, implementing, and making adjustments to the methods and tools incased in this book. Today, my business is a result of their helpfulness in generating referrals and for that I thank them. As well, many of my clients have stayed the course long enough to develop a sales culture and achieve sustainable results which validate the *PowerSelling* process.

I also appreciate the feedback I have received over the years from the sales eagles, especially Jim Salzer, who have not only taken the ideas, methods, and tools presented in *PowerSelling* into the real world, but made improvements to them and shared those improvements without regard for credit or compensation.

My publishing team, Power2Be, was led by my daughter Kelly Power. Her management of this project was of great help to me as I needed to focus on sustaining my business and the writing of the book. I'm grateful for her talent and effort in compiling and managing the critical resources necessary to pull this off.

As well, my family, who has endured over one thousand nights without me over the past fourteen years as I travel the world gathering insights, testing ideas, and working to improve the message each trip. Thanks for your unyielding support.

Where Does PowerSelling Come From?

People all over the world ask me about the origins of the methods, tools, and knowledge I am offering in this book. As usual, salespeople are skeptical; they don't rely very much on theory. They want proven techniques that get sustainable results. It is therefore my obligation, and my promise to you, that the ideas, methods, and tools presented here have been rigorously tested and proven to generate competitive distinction and increased sales.

I have been blessed with a truly incredible profession. As I travel the world training salespeople, I invariably meet the top producers on my clients' sales forces. One of the most enjoyable elements of my job is to get to know these "eagles" personally and listen carefully to their comments, war stories, and even their chest-pounding rants.

I am constantly amazed by these top performers who produce 100 to 300 percent more sales production and thus earn 100 to 300 percent more income than their peers or their competitors. Keep in mind that most of them operate in the same marketplace, with the same products and services, pricing, support, and competition as their peers, yet they transcend their peers and competitors to achieve extraordinary results.

As a result of my fascination with top performers, I have developed a habit of learning from eagles. I make it a priority to spend as much time as possible formally interviewing them, riding out in the field with them, and informally chatting with them during dinner, drinks, or a round of golf. What I find is that they are not 100 to 300 percent smarter than their peers or competitors. They don't work 100 to 300 percent harder. In fact, I find that many like to play as hard as they work.

What I have also learned is that eagles have attitudes, methods, tools, and skills that they have acquired, mastered, and personalized to create their own competitive distinction. Many of them tell me that if they quit the company they sell for and walked across the street to sell for a competitor, their customers would still buy from them because of their professional competence and their ability to develop and maintain meaningful personal relationships.

Eagles are successful regardless of what sales management does for them or to them. They don't rely on their product, marketing programs, or customer service support for competitive distinction. If they are lucky enough to be associated with organizations which provide competitive advantages in these areas, that's icing on the cake.

This book is a result of combining my fourteen years of experience as a salesperson, sales manager, and business owner in the very competitive document technology industry with my experience as an international sales trainer and marketing consultant for the past twelve years. In these twenty-plus years I've made more than 6,000 field sales calls, closed more than 1,900 transactions, presented reams of sales theory, met a lot of eagles, and enjoyed the financial rewards associated with this gratifying profession.

It is my purpose in this book to give you a return on your investment of both time and money. I combine proven sales theory with real-world applications that will generate competitive distinction, increased sales, and all of the related rewards.

CONSULT & COLLABORATE TO GAIN COMPETITIVE DISTINCTION

Above all, there are two behaviors that constitute the cornerstones of *PowerSelling: consultation* and *collaboration.* The word *consult* means to seek advice and exchange views. The word *consultant* means one who serves in an advisory capacity, offering expert advice. The word consult implies collaboration between the person seeking advice—your prospect—and the one who offers expert advice—you. Collaboration means to work together in joint intellectual effort. This means respecting your prospect's interests and allowing each other to participate in the creation of the desired outcome.

You can quickly see why these two concepts are the cornerstones of not only a successful sales model, but any successful relationship. *PowerSelling* is all about the buyer and the seller working together, participating, exchanging, and advising, all with the outcome of creating the desired results.

You will see many traditional sales concepts presented in *PowerSelling* that I agree are proven to be effective in getting sales results. I will also challenge many traditional sales *techniques* that I've seen become counterproductive to the sales process. What I offer are new insights and methods that will help you outperform the many salespeople who still insist on controlling, manipulating, cornering, and hammering prospects.

By transcending these unilateral sales techniques and employing a consultative and collaborative sales process, you will enjoy a competitive distinction that even your products, services, and value propositions can't provide. That is the desired outcome of this book, to help you develop competitive distinction through your own consultative and collaborative sales process.

CHAPTER 1

The PowerSelling Process

Successful selling behavior is the topic of thousands of sales books, seminars, tapes, and sales meetings that have been offered over the past several decades. I've seen dozens of versions of the traditional sales process presented hundreds of times. I've presented it myself thousands of times. I've observed it being implemented all over the world, and I still never get tired of it. I especially like watching the lights go on for rookie salespeople and eagles alike as they see their sales process broken down into a step-by-step sequence of actions that ultimately leads to the sale. There is tremendous value in assigning labels to each step and establishing a common sales vocabulary. This is what enables each salesperson to fully understand and master each step consciously.

I've seen salespeople transcend current performance levels and build explosive sales careers as a result of developing new attitudes, skills, and knowledge associated with a highly effective sales process and the right field sales tools. On the other hand, I've witnessed salespeople learn and implement some *sales techniques* taught over the past thirty years that are unnatural, often insulting, and generally counterproductive to the sales process. Most of these techniques are designed to manipulate, intimidate, flatter, or control the buyer and their decision-making process.

You know what techniques I'm talking about, like trying to build rapport with insincere interest: "Do you fish?" Another technique suggests you *mirror* the buyer's posture and gestures, or even *parrot* everything the buyer says by rephrasing his or her comments with a trial close at the end: "So if I understand you correctly . . . blah, blah, blah . . . Is that important to you?"

The problem with these traditional techniques is that they have been around for decades. Buyers have seen them hundreds of times and are conditioned to them like high-mountain lake trout are conditioned to plastic lures cast by tourists who fish with the radio on. Using these techniques often raises the buyer's defenses, blocks communication, hinders rapport, and in general creates an adversarial relationship.

After decades of being hit with attempted manipulation and mind control techniques, today's buyers desire, expect, and, in fact, demand better from sellers. They want salespeople who are genuine, empathic, and intriguing — people who seek to understand their business objectives and challenges. They need salespeople who are expert resources in their fields and can help them become better decision makers. They strive for personal relationships with other professionals who can help accelerate their efforts to meet their objectives and improve their businesses. In short, they want *advocates*, not adversaries. They want collaboration, not manipulation. They want to participate in the process and not to be subjected to a unilateral event.

THE POWERSELLING PROCESS

Think for a moment about the word "process." Webster defines it as "a series of actions, changes, or functions that brings about a result." For the sake of this conversation, a series of actions and steps in a sales process that brings about a result, the sale.

The concept of process is critical to achieving any desired result, be it the outcome of life-saving surgery, piloting an aircraft, or shooting a successful round of golf. In sales, as in any field, it's important to break down the entire process into critical steps and to identify the elements of successfully implementing those steps. This will help you determine which skills and sales tools need to be developed to prompt and support salespeople in each step. These steps, skills, and tools then need to be linked together seamlessly for a successful outcome.

Let's look at the process of playing golf as an example. The first step in this process is the *tee shot*. This step requires skill (training) in the use of a specific tool, the driver. The next step in the process (besides looking in the trees for your ball) is the *fairway shot*. This step requires skill in another set of tools, the irons. The next step is the approach, or *chip shot*. This requires skill with yet another tool, the wedge. The final step in the process is to *putt* out. This step requires skill in the use of the putter.

The successful implementation of each step is based on certain principles that apply to all situations: grip, stance, head down, follow-through, etc. In the sales process, it's no different. Each step has specific skill sets and related tools that must be mastered. The overall process has underlying principles, which provide a solid foundation for successful implementation.

The majority of this book is dedicated to the *PowerSelling* sales process, a step-by-step progression for bringing about the desired result. The steps are not necessarily new or unique to *PowerSelling*. Nor are they some kind of magic pill or secret weapon. What you *will* find here are dozens of nuances that will help you implement each step with the greatest impact leading to increased sales. There are some unique sales tools that you may have to customize to fit your specific industry. You will also learn "bridge" techniques that will help you link each step to the next. As stand-alone actions, each step, skill, and tool is limited. But when seamlessly linked together, they build on one another, creating a turbocharged effect that dramatically accelerates all of your efforts and results.

PowerSelling is intended to help you establish your own competitive distinction. All of your competitors have their own particular sales processes. It's up to you to have better steps, better skills, and better field tools. At the end of the day, your competence and superior sales process will be your competitive distinction.

Here's a brief overview of the *PowerSelling* process. In the following chapters, I'll break down each step, providing my insights as well as the eagles' secrets for mastering implementation.

Creating Selling Opportunities at the Top

Most salespeople agree that selling their products or services is fairly easy once they get in. Most salespeople also agree that getting in at the top-level contact (TLC) is the hardest part of the job. In *PowerSelling*, I will present three high-impact approaches for setting initial appointments with top-level decision makers. I will present an integrated approach, including targeted mail with telemarketing follow-up, gaining referrals from enthusiastic clients, and gaining referrals from other sales professionals via professional networking.

Pre-call Investigation

This research step is critical for getting to know as much as possible about your prospect prior to your initial sales call. Careful investigation will help you understand what you're walking into, and a little planning will help you prepare to make a good first impression and quickly build credible executive level-rapport. Gaining competitive distinction starts before you even see a prospect.

Relationship

Sales is a people business. Buyers will not buy from you unless they like you personally and trust you professionally. Salespeople must develop the people and conversational skills to immediately create a sense of comfort and trust with their prospects. I will present ideas on how to position yourself as a consultative resource in the first five minutes of the sales call with a sixty-second *positioning statement.* You will then set the stage for collaborating with buyers as an advocate. In the beginning, and the end, sales is all about two people talking business.

Discovery: The Consultant's Due Diligence

Professional golfers walk the course before a tournament, lawyers thoroughly investigate their client's case before walking into the courtroom, and surgeons conduct a battery of tests before operating on a patient. In your discovery process, you will determine your clients' objectives, challenges, specific requirements, current methods, and costs, as well as identify areas where you can improve their business with your solutions. The *PowerSelling* discovery process transcends the typical "qualifying" questions and equips you with intriguing "consultative questions" that will position you head and shoulders above your competition.

The Executive Summary: The Consultative Deliverable

Most salespeople conduct some kind of discovery process. After discovery, most salespeople then deliver their proposal to the prospect. In the *PowerSelling* model, you will package your discovery findings in an *Executive Summary* and present this *consultative deliverable* to prospects *prior to your proposal* or *financial offer.* The Executive Summary is a decision-making support tool for prospects. It provides valuable information that helps them become better decision makers. It also contains

9

your recommendations as to how clients can meet their objectives by implementing your solutions. You then collaborate with your prospects to prioritize which solutions they want to implement. Your prospects participate in your consulting process and thereby take ownership of implementing the proposed solutions. The Executive Summary becomes your step-by-step plan for putting your recommendations to work. The Executive Summary also contains an *Implementation Agenda,* which itemizes action steps required to implement your solutions along with relative dates. The Implementation Agenda helps you "open the closing conversation" and structure the transaction before you present your proposal. This simple document enables you to replace traditional closing techniques with collaborative behavior that will lead to a "pre-approved proposal" and a smooth, predictable closing of the sale.

I guarantee that the Executive Summary and the related collaboration is the missing link in most sales processes. If there is such a thing as a magic pill or secret weapon in *PowerSelling,* this is it. If you commit to adding this one step to your sales process, I guarantee dramatic results.

Propose Your Solutions and Present Your Value Proposition

Based on your Executive Summary presentation, you will craft and present a financial proposal that will justify the costs of your solutions. It is here, in the process—after the prospect has asked you to propose these specific solutions, that you will present your value proposition, unique programs, and services that add-value to your cost-justified proposal.

Collaborate to Resolve Obstacles

Even after careful discovery, a well-crafted Executive Summary, a high-impact presentation, and a cost-justified proposal, you can expect some concerns or outright objections to any of your ideas. It's in this step that you will overcome these obstacles by using your knowledge of objections, references, guarantees, and negotiation skills.

Collaborate to Close

I'll warn you right up front, the *PowerSelling* close is "anti-climactic." Because of all the value you've delivered to your prospect as their consultative resource, closing is simply a natural outcome of your preparation and efforts. The Implementation Agenda you used in your Executive Summary presentation has put you and your prospects on the same page, working toward the same goal, *collaborating* with each other to implement your solutions. I will, however, give you some closing phraseology that will accelerate your closing conversations, all while continuing to work with your prospects in a consultative and collaborative manner.

Expand Your Opportunity via Account Reviews

Account reviews are the key to retaining your top accounts, expanding your opportunity within these accounts, and earning the right to ask for referrals. This ongoing step in your sales process will start the cycle over and over again, continuously creating selling opportunities for years to come.

PowerSelling is not a turnkey, one-size-fits-all process. It is a powerful, proven process that you can easily tailor to match your personality, your industry, and the accounts you serve. I encourage you to take a close look at each step and then use the tools suggested, and examples provided to establish competitive distinction and create the selling success you desire and deserve.

Creating Selling Opportunities at the Top

For many salespeople, creating selling opportunities means personally generating high-quality prospects. In effect, many salespeople act as the marketing and advertising department for their company. They are responsible for identifying and engaging ideal prospects and then taking these prospects through the sales cycle, and in many cases, continuing to manage the customer on an ongoing basis.

There's no doubt that the hardest part of selling high-ticket, business-to-business products and services is getting access to the ideal prospective accounts at the highest level of decision making. Breaking this code is the key to achieving the highest income potential and personal marketability for any independent sales professional.

In industries where salespeople are paid high commissions, such as commercial real estate, insurance, telecommunications, or IT, the commissions are high not only because the complexity of the sale is high, but because the compensation programs in these sectors take into account the salesperson's ability to penetrate ideal accounts from a cold start.

If your sales career dictates that you are responsible for generating your own prospects, this chapter and the next offer you three proven methods for creating selling opportunities.

For many salespeople, telemarketing is the method of choice for generating prospects initially (Chapter 2). From those prospects who become enthusiastic clients, a seller can *earn the right* to ask for referrals. For sellers who wish to multiply themselves, professional networking is another highly effective way to gain referrals from other professional sellers (Chapter 3).

If your sales career does not require you to create your own prospects via the telephone, you may want to jump ahead to Chapter 3 now. If your prospects are provided by your marketing department, you may want to go right to the first step in the actual selling process, which is pre-call investigation in Chapter 4.

TELEMARKETING

Generating Initial Prospects

One night, while walking down one of a thousand airport concourses, I was stopped by a young woman who recognized me from one of my sales seminars she had attended two years earlier. To my delight, she raved about the training, proclaiming that it was the best sales event she had ever attended. My ego was soaring.

After a few moments of accepting her accolades, I asked her how the training had helped her improve sales, to which she responded, "It didn't do a thing." Nonetheless it was the best training she'd ever had. By now, my ego was plummeting fast.

I asked to hear the rest of her story. She explained that she attended the training during the first few days of her sales career at a new company. And while the training on the *PowerSelling* sales process was "phenomenal," she was so new to selling that she had no prospects on whom to use it.

That night, standing in the middle of a mostly empty

airport, I vowed never again to present a sales seminar without first addressing one of the most critical elements of the sales process—how to create a selling opportunity at the top.

I think that most products and services are easy to sell. That's right, downright easy. Many of the wildly successful salespeople I know are not rocket scientists or intellectual scholars. Most have mediocre educations and few professional credentials, yet they derive extraordinary incomes and the related professional status from selling.

One thing we all agree on is that the most difficult part of selling is getting in. The world over, eagles insist they are successful because of their unique ability to create their own selling opportunities; that is, generating prospects. For sellers who are responsible for generating their own prospects, this is a career life-or-death conversation.

Cold Calling Is for Fools

Now, for those of you who were raised on cold calling, and you sales managers who preach this as the cornerstone of successful selling, this is blasphemy. Please, before you go searching for your receipt to return this book for a refund, hear me out.

I'm talking about the kind of cold calling where a seller walks in on a business decision maker unannounced or places a telemarketing call to a "cold" prospect with some rote presentation, hoping against hope to set an appointment with a top-level decision maker. Generally, this is a waste of time and the source of enormous frustration. Only a fool (or just a totally naive salesperson) would set out on a day of cold calling. Now that we've attacked the first sacred cow, let's talk about "warm calling."

Warm calling means you research the business you're calling on before you make any contact with the decision maker.

You might visit the company's web site (yes, you may conduct a cold call to the secretary to get the address!), obtain a copy of its annual report, or search industry databases for information about the organization. Oftentimes corporate web sites and annual reports provide mission and vision statements, reveal current corporate initiatives, and present the current challenges facing the prospect's industry. The financial information contained in the annual report will reveal what kind of shape the organization is in and where it may be looking for areas to reduce operating costs. Many web sites will include news releases revealing the company's latest developments. Corporate web sites, annual reports and industry search services often provide insights that help sellers understand who the key players are on the decision-making team.

Researching a prospect before placing your prospecting call will make you a better informed, more effective prospector. By gleaning relevant information from a variety of resources, you will be able to construct an effective marketing message that is specific to each prospect.

It's Not About Canned Scripts

In the *PowerSelling* model, there is no room for one-size-fits-all, canned prospecting scripts. You must develop a new script for every warm call. You must also customize each conversation to fit the prospect's industry, address the decision maker's objectives and challenges, plus offer solutions that support the organization's initiatives.

The outcome is to make a brilliant first impression by demonstrating above-average intelligence and coming off head and shoulders above your competitors. This is your first opportunity to create competitive distinction. Since many of your competitors will not invest the time and effort to research accounts before they make a cold call, you probably won't even see them once you get in.

I was giving a seminar in Australia and a salesperson shared this example of how warm calling works. He sold digital proof of delivery systems to logistics (trucking) companies. His systems helped customers eliminate the paper chase related to manual delivery receipts, thus expediting payment for delivery of goods, which improved his customers' cash flow. Just before making a warm call to a controller of a logistics firm, he browsed its web site. Under "news releases," he learned that the company had just merged with one of its largest competitors.

When he called the controller, he referred to the merger as an ideal opportunity to reevaluate the current methods of both organizations in the area of proof of delivery. He suggested that this is the perfect time to reinvent the system organization-wide, instead of trying to "squeeze two existing systems together." The controller immediately agreed to an initial appointment to learn more.

Again, the idea is to learn how you can help decision makers deal effectively with current events and challenges and then seize the opportunities that arise from those events.

A Format for Prospecting Conversations

Earlier I mentioned that there is no room in *PowerSelling* for canned prospecting scripts. I do, however, strongly believe in developing a conversational format or outline that will prompt and support you in your telemarketing efforts. This kind of preparation will help you achieve the twin goals of staying focused and keeping your prospect engaged.

In my years of researching top-level decision makers, I have been religious in asking them this question: "When someone calls or approaches *you* for an appointment, what information do you need before you say yes?"

I have defined seven elements of information that, if

properly and concisely articulated, will provide prospects with the answers to their questions, which lead them to say, "Yes, you have my go-ahead to schedule a time for us to talk about this further."

First of all, let's acknowledge the outcome of prospecting by telephone, a marketing letter, or an impromptu face-to-face meeting. Your mission is to first, get the prospect's attention; second, hold their attention; and third, inspire them to act, in this case, to approve the appointment.

Remember, regardless of the delivery medium, you have about ten to fifteen seconds to get the prospect's attention, another ten to fifteen seconds to hold that attention, and another fifteen seconds to offer a compelling reason the prospect should see you for an initial appointment. In a crisp forty-five seconds, you'd better provide the information they require and answer the seven questions they need answered before they say yes. Those seven questions are:

1. Who are you and what business are you in?

2. Do you understand my world?

3. What results do you bring to the table?

4. How do you work? What is your process for engagement?

5. How long does the appointment take?

6. If I am not interested, how can I disconnect gracefully?

7. How can I fit this appointment into my already-packed schedule?

The First Impression

When you call someone, simply introduce yourself, clearly stating your name and the organization you represent. For many of you, your organization's name may help you get the prospect's attention and even identify what business you're in—for example, Continental Laboratory Products, Xerox, or FedEx. For some of you, your organization's name could work against you if it is not recognizable, or if it is confusing, or even obsolete—for example, Omnicom, Rex Rotary, or Portland Typewriter.

I do not advocate being deceptive or clever in proclaiming your organization's name by using initials or abbreviated names, as this just leads to further confusion. If your organization's name is confusing or obsolete, you must deal with that reality. You may say "I'm calling from Portland Typewriter. We don't sell typewriters anymore, but document technology is in our DNA." Now you have five to ten seconds to get the prospect's attention and answer the first question.

1. Who are you and what business are you in?

If someone asked you, "What do you sell?" or, "What business are you in?" what is your short answer? If you are selling commercial real estate, commercial insurance, office technology, telecommunications, computers, or financial services and you blurt out "My name is Silvia and I represent _____ organization. We are in commercial real estate, insurance, or telecommunications, etc.," you have just used three seconds to come across without distinction.

While I will address this issue in more depth under the *Positioning Statement* in Chapter 5, I offer here some suggestions that will help you create distinction. First, you must look beyond the obvious business or industry you're in and define the outcome or result your product or service delivers to the client. Then, package your organization's products and services in a marketing wrapper that's intriguing.

For example, if you sell commercial real estate, you could present your expertise in "professional-space location."

Insurance becomes "asset protection and liability solutions." Printers and faxes could be referred to as "document technology solutions."

The idea is to create intrigue to get your prospect's attention. Remember, the function of marketing is to pre-condition the customer's mind to the sales message, and that starts with creating a perception. By packaging your industry into a wider array of solutions you create distinction. Again, the positioning statement in Chapter 5 will help you tremendously.

2. Do you understand my world?

In other words, "Do you understand my job, my objectives, my environment, my applications, and my challenges as they pertain to the products or services you're selling?"

Here's where it's critical to research your prospect and customize the marketing message to your audience. If you are calling on controllers of construction companies, legal administrators, health plan administrators, or IT directors, you must make a connection between their world and your expertise. You may say, "I specialize in working with [legal administrators] and my area of expertise is [document technology] . In fact, I've worked with other [legal administrators] , including [insert two to three marquee references in their industry] .

This five-to-seven second introduction will answer question #2 and create intrigue. Now your prospect knows who you are, what business you're in, you have expertise in the prospect's industry, and that you understand that world as a result of working with similar decision makers.

Now it's time to speak specifically to whatever it is that motivates the prospect. Before you complete your conversational format, I suggest you compile a list of these key motivators so you can weave strategic and high-impact words and phrases into your message.

For example, CFOs' motivators include the following: controlling operating expenses and total cost of ownership, streamlining the number of vendors they do business with, increasing productivity and developing long-term relationships with strategic partners. Motivators for health plan administrators include maximizing benefits while reducing premiums. IT directors' motivators include maximizing a return on IT infrastructure investments and seamlessly integrating new technology into their legacy systems.

When addressing a CFO, you may say something like, "I understand that people in your position are constantly looking for ways to analyze and control operating expenses, streamline the number of vendors you're doing business with, and increase your organization's productivity."

The point is that each audience has specific motivators, words, and phrases it will respond to positively. It's your job to find out what these motivators are and use them to demonstrate that you understand the prospect's world. Next, you must go a step further and flaunt some specific results you have delivered for other clients.

3. What results do you bring to the table?

I truly believe that this is the most crucial element of your marketing message. You must be concise and compelling in the next seven to ten seconds of your conversation. You must also be specific and believable. In order to achieve this credibility, you must develop a habit I rarely see in salespeople. You must measure the results you deliver to clients and proclaim those results in your marketing message.

A group of commercial insurance salespeople I once worked with determined that decision makers for property and casualty insurance were most interested in three things: identifying liability exposures and expanding their coverage to limit those liabilities, while at the same time reducing their premiums.

I asked the group about their sales process, which included a comprehensive discovery step. How many times did they find yet unidentified liabilities and then develop ways to expand their clients' coverage to limit those liabilities? I also asked if they were able to reduce the clients' premiums at the same time. The group answered that eight out of ten times they achieved this outcome on a routine basis.

Their new marketing message: "Eight of ten times I work with organizations like yours, I'm able to uncover liability exposures, expand coverage to limit those liabilities, and at the same time reduce the client's premiums."

If you understand your prospects' motivations and track the quantifiable results you deliver to clients, don't hesitate to flaunt these results at the heart of your marketing message. Be specific and compelling, and remember that prospects are most interested in results, not marketing hype.

Now you're on a roll. You have your prospects' attention. You've peaked interest by speaking to specific motivations. Now, it's time to inspire action. Remember, the outcome of every call is to secure an initial appointment.

4. How do you work? What is your process for engagement?

Right about now your prospects are asking themselves the classic risk/reward question: "If I spend time with this salesperson, am I wasting my time, or is there some reward for me that outweighs the risk?"

This means that you simply have to provide your prospects with an overview of the initial appointment. What can they expect in terms of value? What new insights will they receive that will help them become better decision makers? What critical issues can you help them address or what new opportunities can you help them seize?

Don't be afraid to use some strong language here. For example, "During our initial appointment, I'll share some insights that I guarantee will help you better assess your current situation and determine if there is an opportunity to . . ." Or "In our first appointment, I'll learn more about your objectives and challenges in the area of _____ and then give you some options to think about and information on how others in your position are dealing with the issue of _____ ." Or "The way I work is to first understand more about your critical issues and objectives. If we establish that there is a foundation for moving ahead, we can talk about taking the next step."

Remember, you're not selling anything here! You're not even selling anything on the first appointment. Your mission is to inspire your prospect to agree to an initial appointment and then decide to engage you further.

You're almost to the finish line. You've been rolling for about thirty-five to forty seconds. Now it's time to answer the final couple of questions bouncing around in the back of your prospects' minds and close for the appointment.

5. How long will the appointment take?

When you schedule an initial sales appointment, how much time do you allocate on your calendar? Be honest. Forty-five minutes? One hour? When I ask top-level executives how much time they allocate for an initial appointment, they usually say thirty minutes.

Remember, the risk/reward question is your biggest enemy in securing the initial appointment. Asking for an hour-long appointment will only beg rejection. I suggest you keep the prospect's time frame in mind and go for a short appointment. You can explain it this way: "The initial appointment takes about thirty minutes. If you want to extend that time, that will be totally up to you."

6. If I'm not interested, how can I disconnect gracefully?

When you go shopping, you usually have a clear idea of what you want and quickly recognize it when you see it. You also know very well what you don't want, no matter how attractively it's displayed. Your prospects operate the same way.

All you can do is give prospects a chance to see the value you bring to the table and determine for themselves if they're interested in taking the next step. If there is no value for them (either you didn't build a compelling case, or there just isn't a fit), then you must offer prospects a way to disconnect without feeling obligated or worrying about you following up every few weeks for the rest of their lives.

At the close of your marketing message, you can make this simple suggestion: "At the end of the thirty minutes, if you see a value in what I have to offer, we can discuss taking the next step. If not, that's fine." It's as simple as that. You're almost there. Just one thing left, and that's close for a date and time.

7. How can I fit this appointment into my already-packed schedule?

Answer this next question honestly. When you suggest a day and time for an appointment with a top-level decision maker, what time of day do you usually suggest? 10:00 a.m.? 2:00 in the afternoon? When I ask this question in sales seminars, 90 percent of the group admits that they suggest some time between 10:00 a.m. and 3:00 in the afternoon. My next question is, why? The answer, most salespeople say,

"That's when *I* can get to most appointments," or, "That's when business is traditionally conducted."

Well then, another sacred cow under attack! Think about it. What are most top-level decision makers doing between 10:00 a.m. and 3:00 in the afternoon? That's right, running their businesses! It's within these same hours that they, too, are fully engaged in meetings and the other myriad details of staying on top. These are peak-productivity times for anyone in business. These peak-productivity hours are the most precious, and therefore the most protected time frames in the day. This means you are faced with mega competition for even a mere thirty-minute time slot.

Based on this reality, I urge you to try a different approach. It's common knowledge that these decision makers arrive at the office early in the morning and stay late most evenings. The solution, then, is to suggest meeting at 7:30 in the morning, before your prospects get into "full stride." You can also suggest meeting at 5:15 in the afternoon, when most people enter their "cool down" period. While this idea may require you to change some of your own personal routines, the results will be well worth the effort. Again, it's all about creating distinction.

Now, simply wrap up your conversation by saying, "I know you probably like to get in the office early or stay late at least a few days in the week. I suggest we get together one day next week either around 7:30 in the morning or 5:15 in the afternoon. Which day and time next week works best for you?"

Here you are at the end of your prospecting approach. You're forty-five seconds into a compelling presentation. You're coming across as well-informed. You're speaking to your prospect's motivations. You're even demonstrating that you understand the prospect's scheduling issues and are smart enough to suggest a sensible appointment agenda.

This conversational format is designed to address prospects' questions and provide the information they require before they say yes to an appointment. It's up to you to customize this template for your business. You can then tailor the content to each prospect.

Blazing a Trail Before You with High-Impact Reference Letters

In training seminars, I am constantly asked if it is a good idea to package this message into a marketing letter and send it to the prospect prior to making the telephone call. Again, the idea of marketing is to familiarize the prospect with your company, product, service, etc., by creating a positive perception prior to the call.

My answer lies in a quick story about an inexperienced, out-of-the-box salesperson I was mentoring in Los Angeles years ago. Troy sold high-end copying and printing systems to attorneys. He quickly embraced the idea of name dropping in his marketing efforts. He also had no problem flaunting the results he delivered to his clients.

Together we drafted a marketing letter that followed the seven-step prospecting format. We positioned Troy as the expert in document technology for lawyers. We added three marquee references, cited impressive results, addressed the specific motivations of the audience (legal administrators), and closed, explaining that Troy would be calling in the next two days to set the initial appointment.

A couple of months later I had lunch with Troy and was delighted to hear about his extraordinary results. He was setting eight appointments for every ten telemarketing calls. When I asked the secret to this astounding success, Troy said that he had "put the marketing letter on steroids." He then showed me the marketing package that he was sending out prior to each call. The marketing letter was the same as the one we developed together, with one small but powerful change. At the end, he had handwritten in red ink, "Don't take my word for it. See what your peers say about me." Included in the package were three reference letters from high-powered law firms, all raving about the results Troy had delivered and the personal service he had provided. Each letter was signed by the legal administrator.

Imagine an 80 percent closing rate in a highly competitive business, where decision makers are shielded with security officers in the lobby, executive assistants, and voice mail.

The answer then is yes, do whatever you can to create a meaningful connection with prospects prior to calling them. I guarantee that if you embrace these concepts, perfect these techniques, deliver your prospecting approach with an air of confidence, and get creative in your marketing; you'll take your prospecting results to the next level.

A Few Tips on Telemarketing

There are at least three major obstacles you must prepare for before you pick up the telephone. First, the delivery of your message is critical to success. Second, you will encounter at least three to four common objections during your conversation with the prospect. And third, you will need to get through your prospect's screening process or voice mail to get to the decision maker in the first place.

Let's Talk Delivery

Many salespeople, armed with a new "script," will sit down at their desks and stare at their prospect profiles on their computer screens, or ponder database lists, or shuffle stacks of business cards while they prepare to work the telephone. With their scripts and databases in front of them, their coffee in hand, and their game faces on, they're ready to "play the numbers game."

I suggest this approach undermines the delivery of the message and compromises the effect of each call until the salesperson's boredom, fatigue, and eventual desperation come through loud and clear. This creates the vicious cycle of the "make more calls" mentality. But making more calls doesn't help; it just leads to burnout.

You can have the most powerful marketing message ever written, but if you read that message from a script, your prospect will hang up. On the other hand, if you have a compelling message and you deliver it with confidence and passion, your prospect will most likely respond positively.

Here are a few strategic tips for successful telemarketing. First, you must know your message. I suggest that you read your draft out loud several times a day for five days straight and time yourself. You should be able to recite this message falling off a barstool after three martinis. You should be able to articulate your message in a maximum of forty-five seconds. By this time you should have internalized the content to the point where you are using your personality to dramatize the message. You should be able to deliver your message smoothly, with proper voice inflection, pauses, and rhythm. Throw in a bit of attitude. You want to sound authoritative yet personable, professional yet casual. Remember, your enthusiasm is contagious!

Once you've practiced your approach several times perfectly, put the draft aside and start making calls. If after three to five calls you start to lose your delivery pace and sink into the kind of robotic delivery that invites rejection — stop. Stand up. Walk around. It helps to use a headset with a long cord so you can keep moving while you talk. Move your hands while you talk. Be as animated as you would be if you were face-to-face with your prospects. Smile when you're talking to people. Treat them the way you want to be treated — professionally and sincerely. Make three to five calls at a time, and then take a short break and sharpen your attitude. Delivery is everything!

A FEW WORDS ABOUT OBJECTIONS
The Fastball, Curveball, and Change-up

Even the best delivery is bound to generate questions or an objection or two. Keep in mind that questions are a sign of your prospect's interest. Likewise, objections are sometimes the prospect's way of finding out more information. They could also simply be misguided feedback based on a lack of understanding. Just remember that all questions and objections are valuable because they allow you to engage the prospect in further conversation and therefore increase your chances for getting together face-to-face to take the conversation to the next level.

The secret to addressing questions and objections is to first, anticipate them, and second, to have an effective response ready. It's the same in baseball. As a batter, there are basically three or four pitches you need to learn to recognize and then learn to hit. You must know what a fastball, curveball, change-up, and possibly the slider look like and then develop the specific techniques necessary to hit these pitches.

In sales, there are three typical objections: Prospects don't see a *need* for your product or service, they don't see a *value* in your proposal, or they are *afraid* of the risk associated with making a decision. You must know how to recognize and handle each of these objections

I recommend that starting today, you maintain an "objection log" at your desk. Begin to make note of each objection you get while prospecting. After a few days or weeks of collecting your objections, take some time to analyze them and develop an effective response to each one. You can categorize the objections into one of three categories: *need, value, or fear.*

Objections based on need sound like this: "I'm not interested. I already have one. We are happy with our current vendor," or simply, "I don't have a need for that right now." Many times this is a legitimate response. In the ten seconds they've had to think about your proposal, they are likely to search their memory banks for conversations or meetings they've been part of where your topic has gone unresolved. Then they ask themselves if this topic is within their realm of decision making. If the answer to these two questions is yes, then they are interested and will ask questions. If not, they will offer the objection.

In handling need-based objections, education is essential to getting the prospect interested in the topic. You must be ready to present a compelling business case for your topic. You may need to explain changes in your industry, the marketplace, technology, or even government regulations that they may not be aware of that require them to reevaluate their existing methods, programs, vendors, and technology.

For example, let's say you're selling commercial insurance. You may have to educate your prospect that in the next twelve months worker's compensation premiums will raise an average of 30 to 40 percent, based on current market trends. If you're selling professional office space, you may need to educate your prospect that, based on current vacancy rates, it's a buyer's market. Rates are at a ten-year low, creating a substantial opportunity to upgrade and expand facilities at tremendous value.

If you're selling fraction executive jet leases, you may inform your prospects that in the next twelve months commercial airlines will be cutting back on schedules, first-class upgrades, and catering. Security lines will only get worse and connection times longer, all of which cuts into their executives' productivity.

You may need to mention your references, saying "Many of my clients like _____ , _____ , and _____ didn't see an immediate need until they looked into how these changes in the industry (marketplace, government regulations, technology) impacted their businesses. Upon closer analysis, they saw the opportunity and now they're far better off."

Also be prepared to educate your prospects on the implications of *not* changing current methods in light of the trends driving their businesses: "What happens if premiums go up 35 percent in the next twelve months? Are you budgeted for that? How will that impact your quarterly results?" Or, "What if you don't take advantage of a buyer's market and when you do decide to expand your facilities, the market is 20 to 30 percent higher than it is now?" Or, "If you continue to fly your top executives on commercial airlines, they'll be standing in longer lines, staying in hotels more, and eventually your most effective people will burn out as a result of the travel."

The point is, you must know what's going on in your clients' industries, marketplace, technology, etc. Wake them up. Snap them out of their preoccupation with startling facts that will *create a need* and generate immediate interest.

Now that you've provided a logical response to your prospects' needs-based objection, don't expect them to say, "Great, why don't you stop by on Tuesday for that appointment?" It's not that easy. Once you deliver your response, be quick to deliver your call to action. Close for the appointment by getting right back to the fundamental close.

Do this by explaining that the initial appointment takes just thirty to forty minutes. If they see a value in taking the next step, you'll talk about that, if not, then not. Next, suggest a day and time.

31

Prospects usually present value-based objections in phrases like, "It's too expensive," "We don't have the budget," or, "We've looked at this before and didn't see that the benefits offset the costs." This is another often-legitimate objection that you can handle simply by educating your prospects.

Your job is to provide information that elevates the conversation beyond the costs associated with your product or service. You must educate your prospects about potential outcomes that transcend your product or service. This may be the added value or a tangible return on investment that clients receive beyond the product itself.

For example, if you're selling commercial insurance, you'll need to equate expanding employee health benefits with improving employee retention and avoiding costly turnover. If you're selling office leases, elevate the conversation from price per square foot to the added value of the prestige as well as the more convenient location for upscale customers that a city-center sales office provides. If you're selling digital document technology, expand the conversation from cost per page to the total cost of producing, storing and retrieving documents. Speak about the costs related to human involvement, office space, and courier services.

If your prospects are currently spending money on a similar product or service, it's your job to bring the big picture into focus. You need to remind prospects that you're not asking them to approve any new expenditure. You're simply asking them to be open to redeploying current expenses and exploring some new options that may lead to opportunities to generate a better return on their investments.

Here again, don't hesitate to use your references to reinforce your value-based education. Explain how other clients you're serving have benefited from at least taking the first step, a thirty-minute appointment that enabled them to make a more informed decision. Then, get right back to the fundamental close. Suggest a time and day.

Fear-based objections will manifest themselves in responses like, "We're not ready to make any changes," "We've decided to stay with what we have," or, "Now isn't the right time." These responses suggest that the prospect has investigated the topic and decided not to decide. Most fear-based responses are based on fear of the unknown, fear of change, or fear of making the wrong decision.

This is a golden opportunity to determine the origin of the concern and present a compelling business case to alleviate it. Here again, education is essential. It requires industry knowledge and market intelligence. It also demands a reservoir of great references who have overcome similar misgivings and reaped the benefits.

Your prospects may present objections related to timing, such as, "We're going to wait," or, "We're going to stay with what we have." In this case you must find out exactly what they are waiting for. Simply ask, "What would have to change on your end to readdress the conversation?" or, "Do you have an event or time frame in mind when you will readdress this issue?"

If your prospect's hesitation is based on fear of the unknown — the economy, interest rates, the effects of a merger, etc. — then a thorough education on your industry and marketplace may be in order. Simply explain to your prospect that you have industry expertise and unique insights on current market conditions that can clarify the issues. Offer your prospect a thirty-minute consultative appointment during which you will provide specific examples of solutions to these particular concerns.

Perhaps the most difficult fear-based objection to overcome is your prospect's fear of change. Changing technology, vendors, business processes, locations, and corporate culture—even changing what kind of coffee is brewed in the break room—are all considerable roadblocks to getting the wary prospect to commit to even an appointment.

Here, education alone won't help. Your most powerful resource is personal testimonies from references. This brings me back to Troy.

Troy's marketing letter referenced clients who had existing relationships with their current vendors for fifteen to twenty years before switching to Troy's company. These clients had enjoyed extraordinary service, great reliability, and outstanding quality from their existing vendors. The letters from legal administrators included in Troy's marketing package acknowledged these existing relationships. They then went on to tell about Troy's unique expertise and the reliability and quality of *his* products, as well as the service support his organization provided. Most importantly these endorsements validated the cost savings associated with making the change to Troy's company. Troy is a marketing genius. He understands that overcoming fear of change starts with reassurance early in the sales process.

To help create a sense of ease and security for your prospect concerning change, use phrases like "maintain order," "migrate toward change a step at a time," and "usher in change as an evolution, not a revolution." Then get back to the fundamental close. Tell the prospect that all it takes is thirty minutes to better understand how responding to industry and marketplace trends can create powerful, positive results. Suggest a time and date to meet.

Always, the key to handling objections when setting appointments or closing is knowing which ones you will face most often and having an effective response ready. Keeping an objection log will help you track the most frequent ones and know which category they fall into: need, value, or fear. You can then be ready with logical and effective responses to each.

Keep in mind that your delivery is just as critical in handling objections as it is in your initial approach. You will need poise and confidence to connect with your prospects and engage them in a conversation that transcends marketing. This requires the human touch, empathy.

You must also understand that your prospects' time is valuable and that you're competing with several other high-priority issues currently demanding their attention. It's up to you to build and deliver compelling arguments that create a sense of urgency and give prospects information that will help them become better decision makers.

One final thought: When handling objections, always remember to conclude your responses with a fundamental close — suggest a time and day to meet. Your prospects will not just open up and invite you in after you deliver your business case. You must, as they say in snowboarding, "nail the landing."

THE DREADED SCREEN AND VOICE MAIL

OK, now you've got your marketing approach down. You know which objections you'll most likely face and how you'll handle them. You sit down at your desk, ready to roll. You make your first five calls. On the first three, you get voice mail. With each call your energy and enthusiasm drop a few notches. You wonder if there are any humans left in the world.

On your next two calls you get a human being — a screen, your prospect's assistant or secretary. You get the sense that you're dealing with a lion guarding a piece of fresh meat. You get grilled with "Who's calling? Who are you with?

What's this regarding?" You realize the screen is processing your answers and making a critical decision about whether your call is important enough to put through. Suddenly, it hits you. Your appointment with your prospect, your sale, and your mortgage payment all lay in the hands of an executive assistant whose mission it is to keep you from talking to the only one who can say yes.

First, let's acknowledge that voice mail is the number-one screening method preferred by most decision makers. It's a reality, part of everyday business, and it's here to stay. You're going to have to learn to deal with it. Second, the traditional human screen has been around for a long time. The higher up the decision-making food chain you call, the more you can expect to run into executive assistants who have enormous influence on who gets in.

My Most Profound Advice Regarding Screens and Voice Mail: Avoid Them!

Many of you won't like this piece of advice because it requires getting out of your existing habits and comfort zones. I referenced this strategy earlier in the seven-step prospecting approach related to what time of day you suggest for your appointments. It works for getting initial appointments and it works for getting past screens.

This approach to avoiding screens and voice mail came to me early in my sales career as I observed the behavior of presidents and top managers at numerous organizations. I noticed these executives arrived to work early and were at their desks every morning around 7:30, having their coffee and organizing their day. I also noticed that between 8:30 and 4:30 these executives were in full stride. They landed back at their desks around 5:00 in the afternoon to wrap-up the day. They left the office around 6:30 p.m.

I began calling my prospects' organizations during regular business hours to get their personal phone extensions from the company operator. I then called prospects directly at 7:30 a.m. and again around 5:30 p.m., only to be greeted by an automated answering attendant. I simply keyed in each prospect's extension number and bingo! They picked up!

The good news is that there are no screens answering prospects' phones during these off hours. Also, prospects are less preoccupied because they are in the middle of either organizing the day or winding it down. Either way, 90 percent of the time they are at their desks, picking up their own phones. You're not competing with meetings, conversations with colleagues, or certainly other salespeople.

I've personally been doing this for years and have trained thousands of salespeople to do the same. Many have validated that trying to reach busy executives during peak-productivity hours is not only impossible, but insane, because it only exposes you to screens, voice mail, and rejection. This off-hours calling technique is guaranteed to work if you are simply willing to change your own schedule to make it work.

If You Do Get the Dreaded Screen

You and I know that screens are trained professionals on a mission. That mission is to identify who you are, who you're with, why you're calling and, based on that information, make the big decision: Is this call important enough to put through to the decision maker?

In my earliest sales experience I rejected the idea of trying to overpower, intimidate, sneak by, or trick these trained professionals. Instead, I implemented two highly-effective approaches. First, I offered the information I know the screen was responsible for obtaining up front. Second, I won the screen over as my *advocate*, versus turning them into *adversaries*.

I know this is contrarian, but think about it. At least 99 percent of the time the screen is not going to put your call through without knowing who you are and who you're with. After that, around 75 percent of the time they're not going to put you through without knowing what the call is regarding. Here's a simple approach: "My name is Steven Power from Sales & Marketing Solutions International calling for [prospect's first name] . THANK YOU!"

Let's look at some nuances. Offering your name and who you're with upfront satisfies the first two pieces of information you know is the required minimum. Next, using the prospect's *first name* sounds familiar and personal.

You want to come across as someone who has been in contact with the prospect before and knows him or her well enough to use the first name. Another subtle, yet profound, nuance is "THANK YOU." Your tone of voice here must be professional yet authoritative. Your attitude should be, "I've given you two pieces of information you need, used the prospect's first name, and thanked you in advance. Now, I'm ready to be put through."

I guarantee that using this simple approach, will usually get you through without the third standard screening question, "What is this call regarding?" If you *are* screened further, you'd better have a good response to this question.

I simply say, "It's regarding an appointment. THANK YOU." I don't say "It's regarding *setting* an appointment." You want your attitude to say, "Look, I'm not the one you want to be screening." Now, half of the time this will work, and half of the time you'll be screened further. (This is a trained professional, remember?) The screen may say something like, "Is this for an appointment that's already been set?" Or "Are you setting an appointment?" Remember, no tricks. Simply respond with "I'm calling [prospect's first name] to set an appointment." If you get a strong push-back here, it's time to switch gears from getting through the screen to winning him or her over as an advocate.

This works because people everywhere are generally helpful if you ask them for help. They like it even better if you ask them for their opinion or their advice. Face it, the screens know your prospects well. They know their work habits, manage their calendars, and are aware of projects currently being considered or implemented within the organization.

The first step, then, is to show a little respect and recognize the screen's considerable position. Ask the screen's name and simply say, "I'm hoping you can help me." Better yet, say, "I'm trying to set a brief initial appointment. How do you suggest I should go about that? What time of day is best to reach him/her? How does the calendar look for the next two to three weeks? Does he/she have thirty minutes in the next week or two, possibly early in the morning, around 7:30, or late in the day, around 6:00?"

I guarantee that by treating executive assistants with respect and by engaging them in helping you, you'll be surprised how many will tell you the best time of day to call back, what events are preoccupying the prospect, and how you should proceed. As a last resort, you may need to learn who else in the organization is a more appropriate, accessible contact.

Turning screens into advocates requires treating them with the utmost respect and professional courtesy. Their world is full of high-powered people trying to get a piece of the boss's time and attention. They will respond positively to a fresh approach that demonstrates executive behavior, versus the old-school approach of manipulative and even deceptive tactics, which only leads to an adversarial response.

Voice Mail

Over the past eight to ten years, due to corporate down-sizing and advancements in telecommunications technology, voice mail has replaced the human shield as the virtual 24/7 screening method of choice.

As a seller, I hate voice mail. I think the person who invented it should be put in an alley with hundreds of sales-people and just a plastic straw to defend themselves. On the other hand, as a busy executive I love voice mail and use it daily to keep distractions to a minimum and maintain my sanity.

In dealing with this dilemma, you'll have to shift your thinking regarding voice mail. Instead of trying to ignore it and hope it goes away, you need to embrace it as a valuable business tool and use it to your advantage. I say this only after you've exhausted every other possibility for personally reaching your prospect to deliver your marketing message.

Think of it this way: If you were an advertising buyer, and I came to you selling a new broadcast medium that would guarantee your marketing message would be delivered, uninterrupted, directly into your target audience's private radio station, would you be interested? Of course you would!

Here's your chance to create that high-impact audio broadcast and deliver it directly to your prospects with deadly accuracy. Again, before you discard this idea, hear me out. First, be prepared. It's amazing how many salespeople leave me voice mail messages, yet blow the chance to make a good first impression by fumbling around sounding surprised that they've reached voice mail! Most of them are collecting themselves and organizing their thoughts as they stumble through the first ten seconds.

Be ready for voice mail. Be prepared to come out strong. Put on your best radio voice and recite your well-prepared and customized prospecting message with a crisp, concise, and compelling delivery. Deliver your message as if you were face-to-face with your prospect. This is a one-minute advertisement. Make the most of it.

Next, make an adjustment to your close by making a request of your prospect. Try this: "As a *professional courtesy*, would you or would you have someone else please return my call to indicate your interest. My telephone number is _____ and the best time to reach me is _____ . Again, my number is _____ . Thank you in advance for this courtesy call."

Make it easy for your prospect by leaving your phone number twice and repeating it slowly. It drives me nuts to have to replay a phone message to capture a number that was rattled off too quickly.

This close is simple but effective. The key words *"professional courtesy"* will resonate with most prospects. Don't be surprised when you get a return call from your prospects or their assistants. I've had many people return my call who have had the voice mail message forwarded to them from top-level prospects. Because of just two words, "professional courtesy," I now have the chance to engage my prospect in a productive conversation.

Dealing with voice mail is all about making the most of this technology and being willing to embrace what other sellers avoid to create a competitive distinction.

ONE MORE WAY TO DELIVER YOUR MARKETING MESSAGE: DIGITAL MAIL

I've had many salespeople come forward in seminars and describe their success at getting through to prospects via email. The key again is to use this effective screening tool to your advantage. First, just getting prospects' email addresses can be difficult, but not impossible. You can often research your prospects' web sites to determine how their company's email addresses are formatted. For example, at powerselling.com you will see, under *contact us*: spower@powerselling.com. This indicates that we format email addresses using the user's first initial and last name. Once you've secured the address, it's time to develop your message.

The challenge in email is to rise above the clutter and spam. In the "subject" box, package your message in a few compelling words that will capture you prospects' attention. Avoid sounding too marketing-oriented. Some examples: Real estate consulting project, Asset protection and liability consulting, Document technology analysis, or Telecom research. Next, make your message as concise and compelling as possible by condensing your usual marketing letter to about four or five lines. This message should answer the seven questions prospects need answered before they say yes, as we discussed earlier in this chapter.

Next, consider attaching a document to the message, a relevant white paper, a current press release on your organization's successes, or a case study demonstrating how your product or service yielded extraordinary results for a similar client. Wrap up your message with the same request you make in voice mail. Request a "professional courtesy" response and include your phone number.

TECHNIQUES, TECHNOLOGY, AND TENACITY

In my travels I've met thousands of salespeople in dozens of industries who are responsible for developing their own prospects. The vast majority of these salespeople have chosen the telephone as their tool and technology of choice in prospecting.

I know that many of the ideas presented here are highly effective in increasing results in generating prospects. I also know that, in reality, the telephone is one of the most difficult tools to master. Using it effectively requires incredible organization and the ability to be quick on your feet in handling objections.

As stand alone tools, the telephone, marketing letter, voice mail broadcasting, email, and making advocates of screens may still yield marginal results. When combined, however, into a "suite" of integrated techniques and technologies, they are absolutely the most powerful way to set appointments with top-level decision makers.

But technique and technology cannot replace personal tenacity. In many cases it will take combining these techniques and technologies with your tenacity to conduct the required three to five follow-up calls before an appointment is finally set.

In my interviews with eagles, I find that this tenacity is the single most important element in their character and behavior that sets them apart. They simply stay in the race longer than their competitors. While their competitors try two times with only one technique then fall by the side of the road, eagles stay focused, keep going, and last longer, creating unsurpassed competitive distinction.

Sample
Telemarketing Approach
for the Medical Laboratory Products Industry

My name is _____ , calling from Continental Laboratory Products, the source for molecular biology tools. I specialize in helping principal laboratory investigators analyze and compare options and control costs related to research products.

I've worked with other principal investigators at UCLA Medical Center and USC's Norris Cancer Center, assisting them in procuring the highest quality lab products for the best price and supporting them with the finest service, resulting in the best overall value in the industry.

The way I work is to collaborate with customers to determine their applications and business preferences. Next I provide product samples and demonstrations, and then price quotations. I then design a follow-up protocol to fulfill their needs on an ongoing basis.

In just about twenty minutes we can have an initial conversation and you can decide if there's a good case for us working together. If you see a value in taking the next step, we can talk about that. If not, then not.

I'm going to be in your building next week on Wednesday morning at around 7:45. Or I can stop by around 5:15 p.m. Which works best for you?

Sample
Telemarketing Approach
for the Commercial Insurance Industry

My name is _____ , calling from _____ . I'm in the business of helping risk managers implement programs designed to protect their assets. I've worked with dozens of risk managers in the manufacturing sector, and eight out of ten times I work with organizations like yours I'm able to uncover liabilities, expand coverage to limit those liabilities, and at the same time reduce the client's premiums.

They way I work is to first understand your critical issues and then share some valuable information on how other risk managers in the manufacturing sector are dealing with those same issues.

I understand you're very busy. I suggest we sit down for just thirty minutes initially and then, if we establish that there is a foundation for moving ahead, we can talk about taking the next step. Since we're both at full capacity during the heart of the day, would you be open to thirty minutes early in the morning, around 7:30, or latter in the day, around 5:30?

Sample
Telemarketing Approach
for the Document Technology Industry

My name is _____ , from Today's Document Solutions.

I specialize in helping CFOs analyze and control operating costs related to producing and managing documents. I've worked with other CFOs in organizations including Mattel, OmniVision, and Geotech to help them identify areas where costs were out of control and productivity was inhibited by their existing technology.

I worked with these organizations to compile a complete inventory of their existing technology, conduct a comprehensive operating-costs analysis, and analyze their applications. I then packaged my findings into a consultative report that helped these CFOs better manage their assets.

I'd like to stop by and show you a sample of one of these reports. If you see value in having one developed for your organization we can talk about the next step. If not, then not. The initial appointment only takes around thirty minutes.

I know you are busy during the day, so how about getting started early, say around 7:30 in the morning, or could we meet later in the day around 5:15?

Turbocharged Prospecting: Gaining Referrals and Professional Networking

I am constantly amazed at how the best salespeople can find the most efficient and cost-effective way to do things. It further amazes me how some can find the easiest way to solve the most difficult problem, like generating prospects.

Many eagles I work with don't rely on traditional tele-marketing for prospects. Many never even send out marketing letters or canvass business parks. Being relationship-oriented, eagles find ways to build *relationships* that generate prospects.

This is not to say that relationships don't take time or involve work. But when we examine the return on investment, it's no surprise that gaining referrals from well-connected, enthusiastic customers and developing mutually beneficial relationships with other top sales professionals is worth the time and effort.

Many people I meet have some referral approach in place. Many are involved in professional networking and civic groups. What I don't see are many salespeople who have a *defined strategy* for gaining referrals from clients or a formal network-ing process in place that delivers stellar results. Following are some ideas that transcend the typical approaches to gaining referrals and networking. They are again based on my personal experience and high-impact ideas I've picked up from eagles.

There's no doubt that the secret to gaining quality referrals begins with building quality relationships with quality clients and delivering knock-your-socks-off service.

Top-performing salespeople earn the right to gain referrals. They understand that they must work hard for their clients if they're going to ask their clients to work hard for them. They leverage their client relationships and personal service into a marketing strategy that becomes a perpetual circle of selling opportunities. Best of all, gaining referrals from clients is the least expensive, highest-impact road to the most profitable prospects.

Take just a minute to think of the potential for new prospects within your current client base alone. Right now, make a note of how many deals you close every month. Next, multiply that number by two. Now, multiply that number by twelve. That's how many quality prospects you could generate over the next year just by earning the right to ask each client for two referrals during the first year of the relationship.

Based on my experience, the closing ratio for initial appointments with prospects who are referred by a close friend or business associate is around 70 percent. Based on this potential, it's obvious that providing extraordinary service and having a defined strategy for turning your clients into enthusiastic advocates should be a huge priority.

GAINING REFERRALS:
THE WINNING STRATEGY & PROCESS

To achieve the maximum results in referral marketing, you must have both a strategy that you implement in selected client relationships and a step-by-step process that will enable you to leverage the potential of each well-connected client.

Let's start at the beginning of the client relationship, which is the point of sale. Traditional sales trainers teach that the perfect time to ask a client for a referral is when you close the deal. While I've seen this work in consumer sales, in business-to-business sales you have not yet earned the right to ask for an endorsement. You have not yet demonstrated your personal service capacity or delivered the results you promised. Why would executives put their reputations on the line so early in their relationship with you?

If you ask for an endorsement at the point of sale, you'll only get low-quality referrals, if any. In *PowerSelling* you're not just going to ask for referrals, you're going to earn the right to get your clients to do some out-of-the box prospecting on your behalf.

A few weeks after the sale is closed and your organization has successfully delivered on the first few promises you've made, simply take your new clients out for lunch or coffee and introduce the concept of *earning the right* to ask them for their endorsement and referrals over the course of the relationship. Begin by asking your new clients why they bought from you. Ask them why they would recommend you, your organization, and your products or services. The feedback you will get is a great morale booster. It reinforces successful sales behavior as well as provides invaluable information you can incorporate into your sales and marketing presentations.

Next, remind your clients that in the process of buying from you, they have, in fact, hired you as their consultant and go-to person on an ongoing basis. Explain how they can best maximize your personal service capacity. Give them your mobile phone number or even your home telephone number with the promise that you are available to resolve any issues at any time. Confirm your commitment to providing "knock-your-socks-off" service.

Now, simply explain the facts of life to your clients—the

realities of the sales profession. Tell them how prospecting is critical to your ongoing success. Tell them that typical prospecting efforts such as telemarketing, direct mail, and canvassing take up about 50 percent of a salesperson's time. Next, tell them that there is no way you can provide them the kind of one-on-one, total-access service you've promised them *and* engage in these time-consuming prospecting endeavors. Yes, you heard it right. You're going to put the responsibility—and the benefits—of prospecting squarely on the client's shoulders. Just tell them that once you've earned the right, you would like to ask them for just two high-quality referrals per year.

At this point in the relationship, the objective is to simply set the stage for gaining referrals. The second step in the process is to, in fact, earn this right. Take four to six months putting forth the effort to deliver on your promises, being available to personally resolve any issues at any time. Nurture the relationship with telephone follow-ups and personal visits. Make an even bigger impact with small gifts of appreciation, such as choice tickets to your clients' favorite events or an outing of golf.

Keep a log of any extraordinary favors you provide that are above and beyond the norm. Keep track of your organization's service history. Calculate and document any increased productivity and/or reduced costs that are related to your product or service. Know exactly what tangible results you deliver each account and package those results into a high-impact account review that you present to your clients quarterly, semi-annually, or annually, depending on your business model (more on this in Chapter 12).

Your first account review should be a love fest. They love you. You love them. Life is good. Now is the perfect time to call in the chip and ask your clients for the favor you staged months ago. After all, you've earned the right.

Remind your clients of the conversation when you presented the idea of earning the right to ask them for just two referrals per year. Get them to acknowledge that in light of the evidence presented at the account review, you've delivered on your promise, and now it's time to request the referrals.

Fasten your seat belts, because here's where I part ways with the typical referral approaches and take the *PowerSelling* approach. You're going to leave nothing to chance. You are going to take total control of the referral process by giving your client specific guidance, assignments, and even follow-up assignments that will solve your prospecting problems for years to come. This will require you to get out of your box and garner some bravado, but I guarantee that the results are worth it.

First, ask for the names of two business associates who your clients know personally. Specifically, ask for the names of top-level executives in similar decision-making positions who respect your clients' business judgment. You may need to prompt your clients a bit by offering some suggestions. Ask them about business associates in industry associations, professional organizations, civic groups, on boards, or even in social settings like their country club.

Other excellent sources of referrals could come from your clients' customer base or even other vendors or strategic partners they do business with. It may be your clients' lawyers, accountants, bankers, or investment advisors who offer the best opportunity for your next few clients. If you're prepared with suggestions, and your client is well-connected in the business community, there should be no problem walking out of the review with two high-quality referrals.

This is where most referral approaches end. In *PowerSelling*, it is where the real work begins. You've gone the distance for your clients. Now it's their turn to go the distance for you. First, you need to get some help solving the screen and voice mail issue when contacting the referral. I guarantee this step will drive your results in setting initial appointments with referred prospects to the 70th to 80th percentiles.

Simply explain to your clients the challenges you face when picking up the phone to call a prospect, even when an associate has referred you. The screen, voice mail, even getting through to a surprised prospect all lead to mediocre results at best. Your solution is to ask your clients for a reference letter of introduction that proclaims your expertise and exceptional service.

Be prepared to provide your clients with suggestions for the content of the letter of introduction. This letter should do several things. It should introduce you as an expert in your field. It should then cite a specific problem your clients had as well as the solution you brought to the table. Be sure it defines specific results your solution provided such as increased productivity, improved quality, or reduced operating expenses. Your letter should conclude with a resounding endorsement from your client.

This next step will turbocharge your success in getting through and setting an appointment with the referral. Simply ask your client to place a quick telephone call to the referral to prepare them for your call and your request for an initial appointment. (I told you this would take some bravado.)

Now the rest is up to you. The next few steps are simple yet proven to deliver extraordinary results. First, craft your own letter of introduction. It should be much like your marketing letter, only tailored to reflect your referral source and the results or solutions you provided them. Close your letter with a request for an initial appointment. Prepare the prospect for your follow-up telephone call in the next few days.

Attach your client's letter of introduction to your marketing letter and send it to the prospect. Wait just a few days and make the follow-up telephone call. At this point your referral sources will have made their call and the prospect will have reviewed your package. After this, getting through the screen and voice mail is rarely a problem. Be prepared to reach an open-minded prospect. Don't assume however, that you'll just waltz in for the appointment. Be prepared for the standard objections and be ready to handle them with confidence.

One more thing—the cardinal rule of gaining referrals is to always let your clients, the referral source, know the outcome of their efforts and thank them, regardless of the result.

I know this is another contrarian technique that requires patience, investing the time to provide stellar service, and conducting effective account reviews. But only in this way can you earn the right to give your clients the assignment of helping you generate prospects. This kind of collaborative sales behavior will also result in creating loyal clients for years to come, in part because it prompts you to conduct account reviews faithfully.

This technique is proven to provide seven to eight initial appointments out of every ten times you try it. I also know from experience and feedback from eagles that once you're in an account where a respected business peer has referred you, the trust level and credibility factor are very high. You enter these accounts with *competitive distinction,* which often translates into much more profitable sales.

PROFESSIONAL NETWORKING: MULTIPLY YOURSELF

Some of you who have joined TIP Clubs, chambers of commerce, and networking groups will roll your eyes and think about skipping this section, and I don't blame you.

Like me, your experience with many of these groups may have consisted of a parade of continental breakfasts with a bunch of wannabe salespeople trading stale information on the most obvious movers and shakers in your marketplace. Even many of the professional networking groups designed especially for business-to-business salespeople come up short on tangible results.

About fifteen years ago, I was sipping a cocktail at one of these insufferably boring affairs when an idea hit me. As I worked the room, I noticed three or four salespeople who had reputations as heavy hitters in business-to-business selling.

Bill was an all-star industrial real estate sales pro who helped expanding companies relocate. Lou was the top-producing salesperson for the largest telecom provider in the marketplace. He had just landed the largest bank in the area, one I had been trying to penetrate for months with no success. Kathy was a top producer for a commercial office space planner. She furnished the space Bill leased to the expanding companies. A client of mine, Jim, was the leading full-service commercial printer in the marketplace. He provided all the marketing collateral for the movers and shakers. Mel was the money guy. He was vice president of commercial leasing at the local business bank that provided the capital for the new and expanding companies.

As I surveyed the group, it hit me that within this herd of dozens, there were four or five eagles who had as clients the companies and decision makers I coveted. Furthermore, I had as my clients the companies and decision makers that these eagles pursued daily. I casually rounded up this group of eagles to run the idea of forming a new networking group by them. I began by asking them what they expected to get out of the existing networking group. They all agreed that the ultimate goal was to get appointments with decision makers. Next, I asked how the networking group was working out to that end. The answer was predictable: "Lousy!" I then asked, "What would it take to make this type of group work for you?"

Their answer was my idea incarnated. Given birth that moment was the foundation of one of the highest-impact, lead-generating machines I've ever experienced.

Bill said it first. "We should defect!" We, meaning the core group of leading producers in our fields. Defect, meaning start our own networking organization without the croissants. I suggest you steal this idea shamelessly.

Creating this kind of high-powered networking system will help you meet people selling commercial insurance and real estate, computers, software, telecommunications, accounting and payroll systems, and executive travel services. The list goes on and on. You'll be surprised how much you have in common in the areas of target accounts you call on and the level of decision makers you pursue.

If you embrace this idea of starting your own tightly knit professional networking group, here are the nonnegotiable elements of success:

Keep It Intimate

Commit to a manageable number of *top* producers. Six to eight is ideal. Remember, it's important to associate with only those who call on the accounts and decision makers that fit your ideal prospect profile. This will naturally limit the size of the group.

Meet Often

Relationships are the key to ongoing success. You can only foster relationships with regular face time. Try meeting twice a month. In our group, one of us would host early coffee or cater a lunch at our facility. As host we were allocated time to present our business, our business model, our client list, and in general inform members about what we do, how we do it, and with whom. Eventually this educational process gave us all the confidence to recommend each other and talk knowledgeably and enthusiastically about one another's businesses.

Have a Goal and a Plan

Early on, we established the rule that at each meeting each participant must bring the names of three current clients who fit someone else's ideal prospect profile. With six to eight attendees, we always had eighteen to twenty-four names to swap.

Determine the Best "Opportunity Fit"

This involves a simple roundtable discussion to decide which prospects best fit which seller's profile. Prospects were then assigned to participants by the referring source or "champions."

Champions Call and Schedule the Initial Appointment

This powerful step is what separates the *PowerSelling* approach from the typical networking approach. In our group, the champions call their clients and set the initial appointments. They simply explain to the client that they have a colleague who is an expert resource in a particular field. They then request a brief appointment to introduce that person so that in the future, when the time is right, the referral knows whom to call for help.

Team Up on the Initial Appointment

This simple step creates extraordinary results. With this approach, it doesn't get much better than to show up at an initial meeting with a prospective client with a champion at your side who already has the rapport, trust, and respect of the prospect.

Your champion knows enough about you and your business to make a formal introduction before handing the ball off to you. From that point on, it's up to you to keep things moving forward.

I have personally experienced the enormous reservoir of quality prospects possible when you synergize with other sales professionals who are committed to building their businesses by harnessing the power of networking. In the past fourteen years I have built my consulting company through many such referrals from helpful clients. I've landed my largest clients as a result of developing relationships with people who wrote a letter, made a call, or arranged a golf outing making sure I was in the right foursome, all on my behalf. I have done virtually no traditional marketing and no advertising. Marketing doesn't get any better or more cost-effective than that.

AN INTEGRATED APPROACH

I have presented three proven approaches for creating selling opportunities at the top decision-making level. Whether you use targeted mail with telemarketing follow-up, gaining referrals from enthusiastic clients, or generating referrals with other sales professionals, each approach takes work and time. As stand-alone methods, each will deliver adequate results. When linked together as integrated methods and practiced on a routine basis for six to twelve months, they will generate tremendous momentum, create a reservoir of high-quality prospects, and keep your pipeline full for years to come.

Sample
Reference Letter
Provided by Enthusiastic Client
for the Commercial Insurance Industry

To whom it may concern,

[seller's name] from [seller's company name] knows our business and theirs. We have found him/her to be an expert resource in the areas of risk management, insurance, and employee benefits programs. I am glad to refer [seller's name] and [seller's company]'s products, services, and programs.

At [reference source's company] we have experienced outstanding commitment, service, and competitive pricing that have surpassed our expectations. Since working with [seller's company] we have realized stellar results, including identifying liabilities exposures, expanding our coverage to limit those exposures, and reducing our premiums by more than 20 percent.

I respect the expertise and personal attention I receive from [seller's name] and [seller's company] and enthusiastically recommend them. By the way, I was happy with my current broker until I saw first-hand what [seller's company] had to offer.

Best Regards,
Referral's Name

Sample
Referral Cover Letter
Provided by Seller,
Attached to Client's Reference Letter
for the Commercial Insurance Industry

Referral Name
Title
Company

Dear _____ ,

Your name has been referred to me by [referral source's name] , who is a satisfied client of mine. I am always honored when someone like [referral source's name] places trust in me by providing referrals.

I specialize in providing businesses solutions in the areas of risk management, business insurance, and employee benefits.

What [referral source's name] has realized is that since we are independent brokers we can offer total objectivity and true innovation. This is due to our access to a wide variety of programs from a wide variety of insurance sources. We also offer the best of both worlds in terms of size. We're small enough to provide personal service yet large enough to have access to competitively priced programs enabling us to provide the best overall value in the marketplace.

We work with companies like _____ , _____ , and _____ . In every case the end result is the same. We are able to enhance coverages, reduce insurance premiums, and improve service!

[prospect's first name] , I will be calling you soon to arrange a brief appointment to introduce myself and determine if there is a fit between what I do and what you want done in the future.

Best Regards,
Your Name

CHAPTER 4

Pre-call Investigation: Gaining Competitive Distinction Starts Before You Even See a Prospect

One of my worst nightmares as a sales manager came early in my career, before I myself had defined and documented all the techniques and doctrine I preach in *PowerSelling*. It started in the car with one of my salespeople on the way to see a new prospect. I asked the salesperson, "What do you know about this prospect?" (Dumb time to ask.) He responded with this vague answer: "He's an attorney. He has a Xerox. I just set the appointment on the telephone and then hung up." I then asked, "What's the outcome of this appointment?" (Dumb time to ask.) He responded, "To find out what's going on."

It was now clear to me, based on the lack of information we had, that there was no use conducting a strategy session in the elevator prior to the call. As far as I was concerned, we were going to a law office to meet an attorney to talk some business. In other words, we were winging it. And why not? We were a couple of seasoned pros. We had pretty much seen it all and were capable of thinking on our feet. Again, this was early in my career. I knew we were cutting a corner in the sales process. What I didn't know was what price we would pay.

The elevator doors opened onto a stunning view of beautifully appointed office suites, glass-walled conference rooms, and expensive artwork lining the halls. Well-dressed legal assistants worked at computers, copiers, and printers.

We announced ourselves to the receptionist. She explained that we were to be escorted to the tenth floor by the prospect's personal assistant who arrived in a private elevator and ushered us in for the ride up. On the way up, I asked her what was on floors two to ten. She casually mentioned that the firm occupied the entire building. It employed more than 100 attorneys, 300 legal assistants, and a variety of related support staff. I'm now thinking that this is bigger than "some attorney using a Xerox."

On the tenth floor, the doors opened to reveal an entire floor devoted to the senior partners, each of whom had a private suite, conference room, and personal law library. As we walked down the corridor, each office got bigger and bigger, until we reached the corner suite, which was well-protected by a huge door with a doorknob the size of a coffee table. This law firm was big. The offices were big. The guy we were going to see was big. And the related opportunity, if played well, was really, really big.

So, there we were, standing outside the really big suite when my sales rep and I glanced at each other just in time to notice the look on each other's face. Here we were, just seconds prior to meeting the really big prospect face-to-face. What's our state of mind? Fear, intimidation, and panic, all due to our lack of preparation. Is this how any salesperson wants to walk into a first meeting? Of course not.

As we entered the suite, things got worse. There on the walls were photos of this guy riding around in a Jeep with Ronald Reagan on the Reagan's ranch. Nearly life-size bronze statues of cowboys, each worth tens of thousands of dollars, stood in each corner of the office. And yes, there was a desk the size of Texas. This guy was big!

The rest of the story is short. We bombed in making a first impression. We couldn't build rapport to save our lives. What were we going to say? "Is that you with Ronald Reagan?" We asked some lame, generic questions, which failed to create any intrigue, and ended up getting politely thrown out within ten minutes. He left us with a definite, "don't bother with any follow-up" attitude.

I share this story because I know it's going on somewhere in the world right now. A salesperson is showing up for an appointment with a new prospect with little or no knowledge of what kind of opportunity they are walking into and will forever blow the chance for a sale.

A LITTLE RESEARCH CAN GO A LONG WAY!

The goal of the pre-call investigation is to gather information about your prospects, their organizations, industries, and current situations. This enables you to personalize your opening lines to build credible rapport, craft relevant and intriguing questions, and tailor your initial presentation to make a high-impact first impression. If you conducted preliminary research prior to making your initial telemarketing call, it obviously applies here as well.

The kind of information that's helpful depends on your business. At a minimum, you should identify whom exactly you are contacting and that prospect's title and position on the organization chart. You'll need to research the answers to these questions: What size business are you walking into? Who else in the organization influences or co-approves decisions? Does your prospect have a relationship with another supplier? What is the scope of opportunity? Is your prospect's organization in a strong-and-steady growth mode or a consolidation mode? Who are your prospect's customers? Who are the prospect's other strategic partners? Do you service any of these customers or have commonalities with any of your prospect's strategic partners?

These few pieces of information, easily obtainable through the most basic research, will help you prepare for the initial appointment and create competitive distinction right out of the starting gate.

Obviously, the Internet has made pre-call investigation incredibly efficient, leaving no excuse for taking this step lightly. Start your research by exploring the prospect's web site. Read what this business tells its own prospects, customers, investors, and the press about itself. Look over the organization's product and service offering. Familiarize yourself with its geographic scope. Visit the "Employment Opportunity" section to determine its growth mode. Scan "News Releases" to find the latest developments, which translate to new corporate initiatives. Use the "Search" function to locate an organizational chart, which will provide information on the organization's decision makers and influencers.

If the company is publicly held, read the president's letter in the first few pages of the annual report. This will tell you what opportunities the company is pursuing and what challenges both the company and its industry are facing. This letter will also spell out the current top-of-mind corporate initiatives and include some internal vocabulary that will be helpful for you to know and use. Don't forget the financials. Is the organization growing or consolidating? Is growth internal (focused on reducing expenses to generate profit) or market-driven (intended to increase sales revenues)? What financial pressures is the company facing? And above all, is the company financially sound? Is its business performance meeting financial objectives? If not, in what areas can you help?

Next, use a database like LexisNexis to learn even more about your prospect's industry, competitors, and customers. Try to determine what your prospect's customers are demanding. Can you deliver something that can help provide those customers with better results and therefore help your prospect achieve competitive distinction in the marketplace?

Other valuable resources include the many fee-based industry analysis and search services, such as IAC Incite. These will offer critical financial and top-management profiling information, as well as related news articles in business periodicals. This information is well worth the subscription fees for the service.

I know it's not always possible, but if your prospect is local, try conducting a "drive by." Drive to the organization's offices or local plant location and check out the building. If it is a consumer-based business, walk through one of the retail outlets or even do some business there. I know this sounds extreme, but you'll be amazed at the reaction when your prospect learns the extent to which you have familiarized yourself with the company.

So what do you do with all of this information you've collected? First, analyze the information and develop comments you can weave into your initial conversation that demonstrate your understanding of the latest developments, trends, and issues your prospect is dealing with. Next, use this information to build rapport and gain professional respect from your prospect. Develop questions on the trends and issues facing the prospect's industry. Be sure to use some of the company's internal vocabulary. Again, the idea is to show up well-informed, make a high-impact first impression, and begin to display your competitive distinction.

IT HELPS TO HAVE A PLAN!

On any sales call you must have a clear idea of where you are going and how you will get there before you ever walk through the door. It helps to know exactly what you want to accomplish on that call and what your next step will be so that you can drive the appointment toward that end.

Before the first appointment, define and document your overall objectives for this account in a pre-call plan. Your goal may just be to get on the prospect's Request for Proposal list, thus securing a chance to compete for the business. Your goal may be to get in and capture the whole bag of marbles or to gain a secondary position to the prospect's current vendor, to co-exist with the current vendor until you can prove worthy of taking over that position. You may also decide that right now it's best to compete for a specific portion of the prospect's business rather than the whole.

Defining your objectives in this way helps you prepare for appointments and stay focused once you get there. Create a checklist for yourself to determine exactly what you want to accomplish on the call, what information you want to garner, what questions you will not leave without asking, what requests you will make of the prospect, and what the next appointment will involve.

I know salespeople who outline this pre-call plan and post it on the inside cover of their pad folios, in clear sight during the appointment. They constantly refer to this plan throughout the call and check off the items as they proceed toward the final goal for the appointment.

It's no mystery how eagles stay focused in those often-awkward initial sales calls. It's no secret how they leverage their knowledge of the account to build rapport, gather critical information, and ultimately meet their objectives for each and every call on their way to the sale. Eagles don't wing it. They abide by these two proverbs: "Failures don't plan to fail, they just fail to plan," and "Success is where opportunity and preparation intersect."

The outcome of pre-call investigation and planning is, through preparation, to walk in with confidence, build executive level rapport quickly, make a positive first impression, ask intriguing questions, and demonstrate to your prospect that you're serious about being hired for the job as a trusted advisor.

CHAPTER 5

Relationship:
It's Just Two People
Talking Business

There seems to be a standard-issue sales behavior world-wide that occurs in the first two to three minutes of a sales call. Many salespeople greet prospects, introduce themselves, sit down, and crack open the briefcase. Then they reach for the brochure, site seller, catalog or laptop, place it on the prospect's desk; and begin presenting their latest product or service, or even worse, their latest promotional program.

Salespeople defend this behavior with the argument that prospects have a fast-paced, get-to-the-point, "What do you have for me today?" attitude, and that they are simply complying with the prospects' expectations and busy schedules.

Let's slow down for a moment and think about what prospects really want. Let's also look at what eagles do in the first three to five minutes of a sales call. As an example, here's a scenario I want you to visualize. Imagine you're in Los Angeles, New York City, Omaha, Paris, Hong Kong, Milan, or Montreal. Over the next ten days you have ten sales appointments, all set at 10:00 each morning. You walk into your prospect's office, and after the usual greetings, what's the first question the prospect asks? Think carefully.

In most every city I've ever visited, the very first question prospects ask is, "Would you like a cup of coffee?" (or espresso, tea, Jamba Juice, or some other gesture of hospitality). No matter where they are in the world, salespeople confirm that hospitality is offered eight out of ten times in this scenario. In many cultures, it's not only common courtesy to offer coffee, tea, or some sort of refreshment upon greeting a guest, it's considered impolite or even insulting for a guest to turn down such an offer.

When I pose this scenario to groups of salespeople in seminars, it's interesting to note that the eagles in the room always accept the prospects' offers while the mediocre or timid salespeople admit that they never accept. It's also interesting that the most seemingly uptight people in the room say that they get offered coffee only one or two times out of ten. Does that have anything to do with their persona when they walk into the room? Absolutely. The way they dress and carry themselves, the vibes they send out in the first few seconds of engaging with another human being all scream, "Let's get down to business" as soon as they enter the room.

Think for a moment about what happens when prospects ask you if you would like a cup of coffee or a refreshment. Usually, prospects pick up their coffee cups, walk from behind their desks and out of the office, leading you down the halls, through their organization, toward the coffee room or cafe. Eagles insist that this little tour is a golden moment in the first two to three minutes of the call to slow down the pace and make a personal human connection with the prospect. This stroll creates the perfect opportunity for small talk about last night's football match, the weather, upcoming weekend activities, or even current news events.

Some salespeople are reluctant to establish *personal* rapport and instead opt to seize this moment to establish a *professional* connection. They will keep the conversation more business-oriented than personal by asking the prospect questions related to their profession. They may ask prospects how long they've been at their companies and inquire about what other positions they've held there. They may refer to some piece of information from their pre-call investigation, such as spikes in the company's stock, a recent merger, or a new branch opening.

Whether you use this short walk to make a personal human connection or a professional one, it can turn the awkwardness of the first two to five minutes of the sales call into a magic moment that puts official business on pause and establishes the instant rapport that becomes the foundation of this new working relationship. It allows you to open communication and build further trust as *just two people talking business* before you settle into your roles as buyer and seller.

As an American, this is an embarrassing conversation. I feel that in the United States, sales has become so professional and so sanitized that salespeople need to be reminded to slow down and accept their prospects' offers of hospitality. In Italy, no business is discussed before an espresso and a cigarette. In France, it's a pack of cigarettes. In Asia, talk of products, services, or promotions are premature before a cup of tea. In Latin America, turning down a prospect's offer for coffee is the ultimate insult and will sour the relationship from the start. For eagles, good business relationships start with two people sitting down to break bread and then talk some business.

LET THE CALL BEGIN

By now you've shared a cup of coffee, tea, a cigarette, or whatever local custom dictates, and established a personal or professional connection. Next, you should have some kind of transition prepared to shift the conversation to the business at hand. You can simply introduce your objectives for your time together. This can come straight from your pre-call plan. You can also review your agenda for the meeting, asking the prospect to contribute their objectives and agenda items as well. Finalize this transition by determining the next step if both of you meet today's objectives. The following is a simple transition format.

Today's objectives:

- Exchange information about each other's organization

- Determine the prospect's objectives and applications

- Explore areas of synergy

- Determine next steps and time frames

This transition statement is simple to articulate. You can say, "It's been nice getting to know you. Let's start out by quickly establishing an agenda for today's meeting. I suggest we begin by sharing some general information on both of our organizations. Next, I have some questions that will help me better understand your specific applications and require-ments. Then we can explore the areas of synergy we have in common. We'll wrap up by deciding what the next steps should be. Do you have anything you would like to add?"

Having a transition statement prepared and being pre-pared to make the first move toward the business at hand is not about controlling the sales call or the buyer. It's a step in a dance, not a move in a wrestling match. When you are well-prepared and proceed with authority, your prospect will be a willing participant in this dance. But, someone's got to take the lead.

POSITIONING YOURSELF AS THE EXPERT RESOURCE
The Positioning Statement

Now that the sales call has officially begun, and it is you who has set the first agenda item, it's up to you to be an example, set the pace and keep things moving forward.

Remember, you are still in the first few minutes of this initial sales call. Chances are good that even if you work for a major corporation or a marquee local organization, your prospect still may not know exactly who you are or what you do. Your prospect may have assumptions about who you are and what you do that may not be entirely accurate. Where many sales people go wrong is allowing the prospect to define them and their value proposition instead of immediately positioning themselves for maximum impact early in the conversation.

I was first exposed to the concept of the *Positioning Statement* by the world-class marketing guru Jay Abraham. The positioning statement is a sound bite that defines who you are, what business you're in, what's unique about your organization or product, what results you deliver to your clients, and how you deliver those results. Your positioning statement will create intrigue and leave your prospect wanting to know more.

I've worked with thousands of salespeople to create their positioning statements. The most interesting definition of the positioning statement came from the salespeople I worked with in Hewlett Packard's Imaging and Printing sales force worldwide. They called it their "elevator speech."

Even with an 86 percent market share, they saw the value of leaving nothing to chance when it came to positioning themselves with their prospects early in the relationship. They articulated one of the most obvious applications for a positioning statement. Here's what they told me:

"Let's say you're on the ground floor of a sixty-story building, waiting for an elevator. When you board the elevator, so does another person who pushes the button for the sixtieth floor. This person turns to you and introduces himself or herself as the CFO of the largest potential client on your 'A' list of prospects. They ask who you are and what you do. Now, it's show time!

"You now have fifty to sixty seconds. You can either look like a deer in headlights and fumble out some low-impact answer like, "I'm with HP and I sell printers," to which the CFO responds, "You should see purchasing on the fifth floor," Or, you can smoothly and eloquently deliver a concise, compelling marketing message that creates such intrigue that, upon arriving on the sixtieth floor, the CFO hands you a business card and says, "That's interesting, I'd like to know more. Call me tomorrow for an appointment."

The desired outcome of your positioning statement is to get your prospect's attention, make a profound first impression, define yourself, and create intrigue. Here's the format for creating your elevator speech:

- Who are you?
  - Your company
  - Your division
  - Your title and role

- What business are you in?
  - What end result does your business deliver to your clients?

- What's unique about:
  - Your company
  - Your products, services, or programs
  - You

- Whom do you do business with?
  - Industry-specific references
  - Title-specific references

- What specific results do you deliver?

- How do you work?
  - Your sales process
  - How you go about delivering results

Let's take a look at each one of these questions and go well beyond the obvious answers to create a compelling message that you can deliver in less than sixty seconds.

Let's begin with, "Who are you?" As I said earlier, even the biggest, most recognizable companies go to great extremes to make sure they create just the right impression in the marketplace, instead of leaving it up to the market to define them. While the question is simple, the answer is not always so. Who are you? What two or three words, beyond the name itself, define your organization?

This first step in this exercise generally results in what is referred to as a "tag line." Your tag line should be simple, compelling, and concise — just three to four words. A few examples: HP—"Invent," Xerox—"The Document Company," and Factiva—"Inspiring Business Decisions."

Even if your organization already has a tag line in place, you still need to define who you are personally — what division you're from and what role you play in that division. For example: "I am with [your organization and tag line] . I am calling on behalf of the [your division] . My role is [your title] ." Again, the outcome is to create the desired impression in the first five seconds. Be clear, concise, and compelling, leaving nothing for your prospects to interpret or assume for themselves.

Next, comes the most misunderstood question in sales: "What business are you in?" I start out most sales seminars with this simple question, "What do you sell?" Some of HP's Imaging and Printing people respond, "We are in the printer business; we sell printers." Salespeople at another one of my clients, which distributes LCD projectors, say, "We sell projectors." Commercial insurance salespeople say, "We sell insurance products and services," and on, and on, and on. You get the picture. They tell prospects what products they sell instead of captivating them with what business solutions their products or services deliver.

Here's an example of someone who truly gets it. I was having dinner with a group of sales and marketing executives at an industry awards function. Seated at the table was the vice president of sales and marketing for Rolex. Someone walked by the table and asked him, "How's the watch business?" to which he quipped, "I really wouldn't know." Then he went onto say, "We're not in the watch business. We sell prestige." He added, "If people want to know what time it is, they buy a Timex. If they want to tell other people about themselves, they buy a Rolex."

You can see from this example why this guy was vice president of sales and marketing. He understands positioning. He gets it. This story clearly illustrates one of the fundamental principles of marketing and that is that *people don't buy products; they buy what the product does for them, the outcome or result of the product.*

When I pose the question, "What business are you in?" to owners of businesses and top management, they usually get it. Rich Raimondi, vice president of Hewlett Packard's Imaging and Printing group says, "We're in the information-delivery business." The owner of the LCD projector distributor answers, "We're in the business of enabling people to give high-impact presentations that will get their ideas accepted." The owner of a commercial insurance brokerage responds, "We are in the business of protecting the important assets that our clients took so long to build and rely on so much."

The mission here is to get your vision and vocabulary into the minds of your prospects. At the end of this step in the exercise, you should be able to go beyond the product, service, or program you sell to clearly and concisely define what your clients are really buying when they decide to do business with you and your organization.

Next is what I call the *"so what?"* question. Imagine during your presentation, that the prospect is sitting in front of you holding a flashing neon sign that says, *"So what? Why should I keep listening?* What's so unique about your organization, products, services, or yourself that positions you head and shoulders above your competitors?" In other words, what is your competitive distinction?

Here's a great way to approach developing your answer to the "So what?" question or *"What's unique?"* Imagine you're sitting at your desk. The telephone rings. It's Bill Gates, Richard Branson, Sumner Redstone, or the most powerful businessperson in your region. They explain that they're evaluating the top ten vendors in your field because they intend to turn over their entire account to one single vendor. Next, they announce that you have five to ten seconds to articulate the *one thing* that makes your organization, product, or service so unique that they would award you the business.

One thing, ten seconds, what is it? What expertise, market leadership, exclusive feature, quality, pricing, support, technical capability, customer-satisfaction rating, or strategic partnerships put you far ahead of the pack? Maybe it's you, your reputation, your commitment to service, or your personal expertise that your competitors just can't match.

Remember, your positioning statement is a microwaved version of your full-blown presentation. Keep this element concise and compelling in order to assure the highest impact.

You're now about a third of the way into your sound bite. You sound intelligent and intriguing, far better than the last several salespeople this prospect has seen this week. Now, it's time to kick in the turbocharger. You need to answer the prospect's next two questions: "Why should I keep listening?" and even more importantly, "Why should I consider engaging you as my consultative resource?" Here's where you do some name-dropping. Announce the names of your best marquee clients and state the results that your product, service or program enabled them to realize. Be specific and quantifiable where possible.

I experienced the power of references and results while working with a client to put together a very large transaction in my sales consulting business. Before the client would commit to an initial licensing agreement for the *PowerSelling* process and related tools, he wanted proof that the methods would generate more profitable sales.

The client tested *PowerSelling* by implementing it in a few key branches and then carefully measuring results, including new appointments, proposals delivered, sales won, and profit margins on sales. Measuring the impact of the program and identifying a quantifiable return on investment led to the phasing in of the program worldwide over two years. By the way, measuring results also led to the client's endorsement on the back cover of this book by Mr. Kirk Yoshida of Ricoh Corporation.

One thing I learned from this experience was to measure and quantify results and then to proclaim those results in the heart of the marketing message. When you can point to quantifiable outcomes of your products, services, expertise, or programs, and when the prospect recognizes you as the best resource for achieving similar results, you move up in your positioning from a wannabe to a player. You move from intriguing to compelling.

Now you're well into your positioning statement and you have ten to fifteen seconds left. It's time to provide a brief explanation of how you work. Tell the prospect about your process for engaging similar clients, determining their requirements, and consulting and collaborating with them to drive the desired results.

It's really quite simple. Just explain your consultative sales process from start to finish. It may sound something like this: "The way I work is to first invest some time assessing your requirements, your current situation, and your objectives and challenges. Then, I package and present my findings of that discovery process into an Executive Summary, where I make a series of recommendations. Next, I collaborate with you to determine which recommendations you want to implement. I then offer a proposal and an implementation plan. With your approval, we work together to implement the solutions. Finally, I commit to measuring results and assisting you in managing the project on an ongoing basis to assure that you achieve the maximum return on your investment."

So there you have it, an elevator speech that positions you in the prospect's mind as an expert resource who is intriguing and compelling, focused on results, and — how refreshing—a salesperson with a logistical process for driving long term results! For maximum effectiveness, keep it simple, concise (sixty seconds maximum), and compelling (no hype). As with your prospecting script, your positioning statement has to be delivered with poise and confidence.

In my work, helping hundreds of clients create their positioning statements, I am always amazed at how profound this exercise is. Beyond a powerful sales tool, this positioning statement often becomes the cornerstone of all sales presentations, marketing collateral, advertising content, prospecting letters, and telemarketing scripts.

Keep in mind, it's now just five minutes into the first sales call. You've built rapport, made a transition to the business at hand, and positioned yourself in the prospect's mind as a player with a process. Now it's the prospect's turn. Your first agenda item was to "share some information about your organizations." You just did that. Now invite the prospect to do the same. You may want to take the lead by offering some questions that mirror your positioning statement. For example, you may ask, "What is the final outcome of your product, service, or programs that your customer is looking for? What's unique about your organization? What results do you deliver for your clients, and how do you go about delivering those results?" Simply engage the prospect in briefly explaining their business model.

After your prospect is finished, acknowledge the value of the information exchange and make your transition to the next agenda item, which is to begin the discovery process. For some salespeople, the discovery process is short and simple, and can be conducted here and now. Other salespeople, with more comprehensive discovery processes will simply present an overview of their discovery process with the outcome of gaining the prospect's approval for this in-depth investigation in the near future.

If you embrace the *PowerSelling* process and document your discovery findings into an *Executive Summary,* you will need to present a *sample* Executive Summary report to your prospect at this time. A quick overview of a well-crafted Executive Summary will validate your consultative process and reinforce its value as a decision support tool for the prospect. If presented well, the sample Executive Summary will inspire your prospects to engage you as their consultant and even endorse you within their organizations with the outcome of producing a similar consultative deliverable for them.

The outcome of this sales call is to stage the next step in the *PowerSelling* process, which is discovery. Your ability to establish rapport quickly, position yourself as an expert resource, and provide a consultative deliverable that helps your prospect be a better-informed decision maker will result in your gaining complete access enterprise wide with the decision maker as your champion.

Sample
Positioning Statement
for the Medical Laboratory Products Industry

Continental Laboratory Products (CLP) is your source of tools for molecular biology. I am your product specialist and expert resource for over 2,300 products.

CLP is in the business of helping laboratories maximize and expedite quality research most cost effectively.

What's unique about CLP is that we are the inventors, manufacturer, and distributor, all under one roof. As inventors, we are the innovators who set the industry's standards for quality. As a manufacturer, we deliver the best quality via our state-of-the-art manufacturing facility and quality control programs. As the distributor, we provide the best overall value and save you money by cutting out the middle man. Plus we offer the highest possible responsiveness due to our immediate access to our own inventory.

CLP is a major supplier to the National Institute of Health. We've manufactured custom products for the Center for Disease Control. Locally, we work with UCLA and USC medical centers.

The result we deliver to customers is the best overall value in managing their laboratory materials so they can focus on producing quality research.

The way I work is to collaborate with you to determine your needs and applications and then present and propose products and programs specific to your lab. Next, we can establish a protocol for fulfilling your needs and following-up on an ongoing basis.

Sample
Positioning Statement
for the Document Technology Industry

Today's Office Solutions in the business of helping organizations achieve business efficiencies and cost savings as a result of better managing their documents and the related technology.

We specialize in consulting with organizations to evaluate and control their operating costs associated with the production, management, and distribution of documents.

We've worked with companies like _____ , _____ , and _____ to help them identify their objectives and challenges in managing document technology. We also help them gain an understanding of their workflow processes, device populations, and total cost of ownership.

Our unique consulting process allows us to collaborate with our clients to identify areas in which they can harness new technology to increase productivity, while reducing costs. Based on our expertise and technology, we can recommend innovative solutions leading to measurable and sustainable results for years forward.

If this sounds like something you're interested in, I have a brief presentation on our consulting process and some sample deliverables that will help you determine if what I do would be of value to you. If it looks like something you'd like to pursue, we can talk about taking the next step.

Sample
Positioning Statement
for the Commercial Insurance Industry

[your company] is in the business of providing solutions in the areas of risk management, business insurance, and employee benefits. We are a leading resource for insurance and benefits programs from world-class providers such as USF&G, Fireman's Fund, Kemper, and Hanover, to name just a few. We offer property and casualty, liability, Worker's Compensation, Employee Practices Liability, and director's and officer's insurance combined with comprehensive employee health benefits programs.

What's unique about our company is that since we are independent brokers, with access to such a wide variety of programs from such a wide variety of insurance companies we can offer total objectivity. We also offer the best of both worlds in terms of size. We're small enough to provide personal service, yet large enough to have access to competitively priced programs. This allows us to provide the best overall value in the marketplace.

We've worked with companies like _____ , _____ , and _____ . In every case the end result was the same. We are able to enhance their coverages, reduce their insurance premiums, and improve their service!

Our initial consultation process includes a discovery phase to determine your applications and a comprehensive costs analysis. We then produce an executive report that will either validate that you're managing your risk and employee benefits programs most cost effectively or reveal areas you could improve coverage, service, and perhaps reduce expenses.

Sample
Positioning Statement
From the Sales & Marketing Solutions
International Web Site

Sales & Marketing Solutions International is in the business of helping business clients grow their bottom line by feeding their top line.

We accomplish this by providing expertise and solutions in three areas:

- **THINK.** Go to market strategy—determining who sells what and where

- **PowerSelling.** Advanced consultative sales training—defining and documenting your sales process

- **SalesWare.** Customized sales process software tools that prompt and support your salespeople in implementation

S&MSI is unique because we approach consulting as a process and not an event. Our goal is to fully understand our client's unique objectives and challenges then customize all consulting and training to meet those objectives and fit into the client's existing sales culture. We accelerate results by integrating the client's marketing strategy and sales process and providing software tools and implementation support to sales people.

— CONTINUED

Our clients realize quantifiable results that include increased sales revenues and profits, reduced turnover, and the enhancement of sales managers' and salespeople's lifestyles.

S&MSI has international references with market leaders including Hewlett Packard, Ricoh, Canon, America Online's Digital City, Hitachi, Sharp, and various members of the Young President's Organization.

Our engagement process includes an exploratory interview to determine if a full opportunity analysis and sales force assessment is appropriate. Based on our findings, we work with you to propose customized recommendations for implementation and ongoing reinforcement.

CHAPTER 6

Discovery:
The Consultant's Due Diligence

The needs-assessment step in the sales process is one of the longest-running traditions in the sales profession. It is at the heart of sales training programs delivered worldwide. In fact, sales training in this area is so similar from industry to industry that I can go anywhere and ask salespeople to recite the "standard-issue" questions they ask to determine the prospect's needs or, as many put it, to *"qualify"* prospects.

These *qualifying* questions are usually served up in the first five minutes of the first sales call and are designed to determine the prospect's needs, decision-making time frame, budget, and decision-making authority. Standard-issue qualifying questions usually include the following:

- What is your volume or usage level of this product?

- What kind of service program are you on, and what's included?

- What are you currently paying for this product or service?

- What is your time frame for making a decision?

- How often do you order this product or service?

- Who else besides yourself is involved in the final decision?

- What are your requirements or special needs?

- What problems are you experiencing?

There are many more questions that salespeople ask, but I think you'll agree that most salespeople in your marketplace are asking the same, basic needs-determination and qualifying questions, leaving little room for competitive distinction during this stage in the sales call. That's what I will challenge in this chapter.

First, let's be clear: I agree that fact-finding questions, regarding the prospects' needs, time frame, budget, and authority are important to your sales process, and I'm not suggesting that you throw them out completely. My point is, they're not appropriate in the first five to ten minutes of the first sales call with a top-level executive. Because these detail questions are usually not intriguing, top-level people will become easily bored and you'll quickly be relegated to purchasing or to lower-level decision makers.

I believe you can and should create competitive distinction in every phase of the sales process. I also believe that your discovery process offers a perfect opportunity to get out of your box and ask some intriguing questions that your competitors probably aren't asking and that your prospects aren't expecting.

Top executives are visionaries and conceptual thinkers. They live in and think about the big picture. Many of them refer to this as viewing the world "from 40,000 feet." In order to create competitive distinction at this level, you'll need big, intriguing questions that will capture their attention and hold their interest. You'll need questions that will cause prospects to stop and think through their answers.

A LITTLE HISTORY

Before I started my consulting business, I had no idea what consultants did, what the consulting process looked like, or what consultative questions were. I figured that consulting was where guys like me ended up in a mid-life, mid-career crisis— a kind of professional purgatory. I imagined a waiting room where you hung out until you decided what you wanted to do when you grew up or got a real job, whichever came first. In the meantime, if someone asked what I did, I could always say, "I'm a consultant."

In my early research of the consulting business, I learned that 95 percent of consulting businesses went out of business in the first two years. This information scared me to death. It also prompted me to seek out and attend several seminars offered by some former Big-Eight consultants who, for some fat fees, helped people like me start and build consulting businesses.

After attending three or four of these seminars, I realized that consultants are trained in standard-issue *consultative questions* just as salespeople are trained in standard-issue *qualifying questions*. The big difference is that consultative questions are not designed to qualify prospects, they're designed to define the prospects' big picture, their frame of reference, overall business strategy, current business initiatives, and challenges in implementing their strategies. In short, they are designed to define the view from 40,000 feet.

CONSULTATIVE QUESTIONS: THE VIEW FROM 40,000 FEET

The first three standard-issue *consultative questions* that consultants are trained to ask are, "What are your objectives?" "What are your challenges meeting those objectives?" and "What is the impact to your organization if those objectives are not achieved?" I'll get to exactly how to ask each of these questions in a few moments, but first let's acknowledge that these decision makers are objective-oriented people.

Top-level executives eat, drink, and sleep their objectives. They are constantly focused on the outcomes that they are personally responsible for delivering. Top-level people also recognize their challenges and problems a mile away. They also understand that there are consequences for not over-coming these challenges and delivering the desired results.

If you ask a "C-level" executive what their objectives are in the area of [your expertise] , don't be surprised if they come back quickly with clearly defined and quantifiable goals that they are committed to achieving, complete with dead-lines attached. When you ask, "What challenges are keeping you from reaching these objectives?" don't be surprised if they rattle off two to three problems without second-guessing your question.

If you want to position yourself as a consultative resource to your prospects, get to know what they're trying to accomplish (their objectives), what's keeping them from accomplishing their objectives (their challenges), and what the ramifications are (both negative and positive) if they meet or don't meet their objectives.

MORE 40,000-FOOT QUESTIONS

Once you've asked the three standard-issue consultative questions, stay at the 40,000-foot altitude and continue to develop a clear understanding of the big picture.

Ask your prospects about their organizations' current business initiatives. These are specific projects currently being implemented throughout the organization. Examples are

Supply-Chain Management, Customer Relationship Management, and Sales Force Automation, to name just a few. Other examples may include cost-cutting programs, consolidation of workforces, shedding non-core business centers, expanding sales into international markets, and launching new products or services.

Other questions that will help you gain insight into the big picture include:

- What significant changes are being made in your business model?

- What are the top trends forcing you to examine the way you do business?

- What strategic partnerships have you developed to assist you in meeting your objectives?

- Which of these partnerships are most unique and powerful and why?

- What pressures are you responding or reacting to?

- What are the driving forces being discussed in your management meetings?

There you have it. Asking questions about objectives, challenges, impacts, initiatives, changes to the prospect's business model, trends, and strategic partnerships will give you a clear picture of what's going on at 40,000 feet. By asking consultative questions, you not only capture information that helps you determine how you can help your prospects, but you also get their attention and hold their interest, creating competitive distinction. If you've implemented your consultative questions well, your prospects are now saying to themselves, "Finally, a salesperson who gets it at my level, someone who understands my world."

DISCOVERY FROM 20,000 FEET

Now, what about the view from 20,000 feet, the mid-management level? In most business-to-business sales environments, the decision making is shared among multiple management team members. At the very least, decisions are influenced at multiple levels of the organization. Mid-level and regional managers are often asked by top management to provide input to decisions that affect the manager's scope of authority.

Mid-level managers are implementers of overall corporate strategy on a local level. They know the organization's objectives, challenges, and major initiatives, but where they live their days is in the implementation of *tactics*. They focus on processes and methods that, when combined with other division managers' implementations, achieve the corporate objectives. Once you've established the big picture, you need to go deeper and wider within the account to get the 20,000-foot view from these implementers. This requires a subset of discovery questions that allows you to gather critical information to help you identify even more areas in which you can provide solutions for the prospect.

When you get in front of department, division, or regional managers, you will have to adjust the way you phrase your consultative questions to better relate to this audience. I'm not talking about dumbing down the questions, but rather relating the questions to their world. Let's take a look at the same consultative questions we asked top executives, now rephrased for mid-level managers.

Again, it's critical that you ask the consultative questions in relation to your specific area of expertise. For example, if you're selling IT, you would ask the IT manager, "In managing your network infrastructure, what are your objectives?" If you're selling outsourced payroll services, you would ask the finance manager or controller, "When it comes to managing your payroll activities, what are your challenges?" And if you're selling employee benefits insurance, you would ask the human resources manager, "In managing your employee benefits program, what are your objectives and challenges?" Your questions reflect that you are there to help your prospects better manage the functions that your expertise, products, and services support.

To determine the trends impacting change in your prospect's department or the initiatives currently being implemented, simply ask, "What are the major initiatives that are currently being implemented in your department?" or, "What business trends are causing you to change the way your department operates?"

Being implementers of tactics, processes, and methods gives mid-level managers an intimate knowledge of information, including: current methods; specific applications; requirements; and satisfaction levels with current methods, technology, and vendors. While interviewing departmental managers, you can also identify service problems, costs overruns, delivery problems, desired improvements, expectations from vendors, and what factors would inspire them to change vendors. Five to six consultative questions combined with your current discovery questions should be sufficient to determine the view from a 20,000-foot implementation level.

DISCOVERY QUESTIONS AT THE GROUND LEVEL
Wandering Around

Depending on the nature of your product or service, you may need to expand your discovery process to include interviews with end-users or work-groups. This will help you determine specific applications and requirements as well as identify even more areas you can improve and problems you can solve. This is discovery at the ground level. Some of the best salespeople I know insist that *"wandering around,"* asking questions, is the most powerful step in the discovery process. They get out in the real world, talk to real people, and get real information, information that even mid-level managers often can't provide or aren't aware of.

There's no doubt that these *site surveys* can take time and include a lot of work. You should be well prepared with pre-arranged appointments with work-group managers, a list of specific questions, a checklist of information to be gathered, and in some cases even a digital camera and dictation device to document conditions and record observations.

I've personally been out on site surveys with salespeople who sell commercial insurance, telecommunications, medical laboratory products, office and network technologies, commercial real estate, and even pet supplies! It is absolutely incredible to see the wealth of information and business issues that become obvious when you're wandering around in the real world, talking to people, looking at facilities, and learning how your prospects' businesses operate on a daily basis.

What becomes obvious when you're wandering around are the vast opportunities for you to improve your prospects' business processes with your expertise, technology, products, and services. Whatever field you're trained in, you'll find areas you can improve, systems you can redesign, problems you can solve, and expenses you can reduce or eliminate. You'll quickly see that many companies piece together their current methods based on very little investigation by either their current vendor or even their own internal resources.

Successful site surveys require sponsorship from the top, pre-arranged logistics, extreme personal organization, and time. If you're an expert in your business and you become an expert in your prospect's business, if you know what you're looking for and you're willing to walk around with your eyes and ears wide open, you'll see opportunity after opportunity fall in your path.

So far I've presented three levels of discovery. First, I offered visionary, intriguing consultative questions for top-level decision makers to help you get the big picture. Second, I gave you a mix of consultative questions and discovery questions regarding applications, requirements, and logistical details for mid-level managers. Third, I introduced you to the concept of the site survey, visiting end-users and work-groups to get a ground-level understanding of daily applications, problems, and opportunities for improvement. Let's take a look at some methods for combining these discovery steps and staying organized along the way.

THE "F" WORD

When I work with sales organizations to help them define and document their consultative sales process, first we list six to eight consultative questions for the top-level contact. Next, we list and arrange, in logical order, the mix of consultative and discovery questions for mid-level managers. Then, we design the field questions for the site-survey.

When combined, all these questions are formatted into a document that some call the "F" word: a *"form."* I refer to this document as the *account profile*. This profile is a field tool that will prompt and support you in consultative discovery and documenting each prospect's business environment. It will be your blueprint for building your selling strategy, Executive Summary, sales presentation, and proposal. The account profile will eventually serve as your roadmap for closing the sale. It is a dynamic tool in that it is completed in stages as you go through your consultative sales process.

At this point I strongly urge you to make a list of questions, format them onto a document, or form, and prepare to implement this tool in your discovery process. Now I know from my personal experience as well as from training thousands of salespeople that there is a real need to look cool and in control during sales calls. The thought of pulling out a form in front of a prospect and asking questions from a list sounds unnatural and uncool, and many salespeople will dismiss the very thought of it as too clinical.

What are your chances, however, of remembering five to seven great consultative questions, plus another seven to ten discovery questions, asking them in an organized flow, staying focused, and remembering all of your prospect's answers after the appointment? So how do you look cool, yet in control, and stay organized and focused at the same time? Let's first look at the challenge of looking cool and in control.

Imagine that you have an appointment with your attorney to discuss an important legal matter. You're paying $250 an hour for this conversation. What would you think if the attorney asked you seven or eight questions in a seemingly random manner and didn't take notes? Then imagine your attorney asking another eight to ten questions in no particular order, backtracking through your previous answers, and jumping in and out of context, occasionally jotting down a few partial notes.

What would be your impression? What would be going through your mind? Is this attorney interested? Is he or she professional, thorough, organized? Is he or she worth $250 an hour?! What if this happened on an appointment with your accountant at tax time or your physician during a critical physical exam? You would no doubt have the same questions and misgivings.

To determine the prospect's impression of this discovery tool, my organization has interviewed customers who have been in meetings with salespeople who worked from their account profiles. The prospects' responses were consistently positive. They said things like, "The salesperson appeared professional and seemed interested in my business," "The appointment had a nice flow to it," and "The salesperson was well organized."

There definitely needs to be a balance here. Obviously you don't need to walk in with a white smock and a form attached to a clipboard. You also want to avoid diminishing the personal connection you've created by quoting questions from a list and then dropping your head, losing eye contact, and clinically recording your answers on a form. Be very careful in designing your field tool so that you don't limit yourself to staying within small boxes and confining lines. Your profile doesn't need to have the entire question written out, just a couple of key concepts to prompt you to articulate the question in your own style.

Position the account profile on the inside of your pad folio. When you begin asking the questions, casually open your folder and begin recording your findings. Once you know your questions well, all you need to do is conversationally articulate them and record the answers using the profile as a prompter to stay on course. Don't be afraid to tell the prospect that you have some questions listed and you'll be taking some notes. Your prospect will be impressed by your preparation and diligence.

COMMUNICATION 101: LAYERING QUESTIONS

Years ago I was in a conference facilitated by management consultant Mike Riordan. He casually mentioned that he was going to give us a "clinic" in a simple communication technique that, as he put it, "will change your life." I started out a bit cynical, but I knew Mike and trusted this Midwestern sage, so I was open-minded to the life-changing technique he presented.

This is no magic pill or silver bullet, as Mike put it, but WOW!—what a difference it makes in getting your prospects to open up, expand on their answers, and offer ten times the information that the untrained salesperson can only hope to get.

You've heard about "peeling the onion." This is a simple form of that. Mike calls this technique *"layering questions."* It's a form of *therapy,* with the outcome of getting to the heart of the matter in any conversation. You know as well as anyone else that most people hold conversations on a first-level (first-layer) basis. When you get into a cab, board an elevator, get to work in the morning, or go home at night, what's the first thing you say to the cabbie, your coworkers, or your wife, husband, kids, dog? "How was your day?" It's a simple question. How do they respond? "Fine," "Great," or "Not bad." This is a *first-layer* answer, the easiest, most obvious answer. It requires no thinking whatsoever. As a result, first-layer answers seldom provide any accurate or meaningful information.

Any one of these people, in fact, may have had a terrible day. Perhaps the kids set the garage on fire, the cat got run over, or the mother-in-law called and is coming for a visit. They may have the flu or any number of things going on that are not "fine," "great," or "OK." The problem with first-layer answers is that most people accept them and move on to the next question or provide a simple acknowledgment in return. This only results in a shallow and meaningless conversation.

In a sales call, you may ask a Chief Financial Officer, "What are your objectives when it comes to managing your _____?" (budgets, vendors, insurance, properties, etc.). The *first-layer answer* is generally, "to reduce costs and save money." This is the easiest, most obvious answer that any CFO is likely to give. Most salespeople will record this answer and move to the next question. By "layering" your questions or getting your prospect *"into therapy,"* you can get beyond this limited answer to the heart of the matter. The idea is to get people to really think about the question and provide answers that go beyond the obvious.

Here are a few simple phrases that will inspire your prospect to go to that next layer:

- "Tell me more about that."
- "Give me an example of _____."
- "In addition to that, what else?"
- "Let's explore that. Please go on."
- "Go on, tell me more."

In the example above, when the CFO says, "My objective is to reduce costs and save money," many salespeople immediately think, "To get this business I have to discount my price and come in below what the prospect is currently paying."

Here's a perfect application for layering the question: *"Tell me more about reducing costs, specifically in the area of _____ (telecom, printing, insurance, etc.). What are you thinking?"* The second-layer answer may be, "We currently deal with five vendors and we're not leveraging our buying power. Plus, it costs us a fortune to have ten divisions evaluating their own requirements, negotiating their own contracts, and administrating their own vendors. By consolidating purchasing and single-sourcing our contract, we think we could save some money." Wow! Now it's time to get to the third layer.

Next, you can say, *"In addition to saving money and consolidating vendors, what are some of your other objectives?"* This is the third layer, you're getting to the heart of the matter. The response may be, "Well, another objective is to ensure that we get the highest-quality products and the best-possible service and support."

Now, you say, *"Go on. Tell me more."*

"We don't want to compromise on quality to save money.

We need to support our people with the best possible tools and make sure that the quality of our products and services isn't compromised."

Here, we are finally at the core issue. At this point, it's obvious that your job is not selling price, but selling vendor consolidation, quality, and service. In other words, you are in front of someone who understands *"value."*

I guarantee that layering questions will change your sales life enormously. You will capture so much valuable information that it will amaze both you and your prospect. Getting down to the inner layers of information will help you improve your strategy, proposals, and presentations, beyond what any form of price discounting will ever provide.

Be careful with layering questions, however. As with any technique, you can overuse it. Too much intense digging will become tedious to your prospect, making it counterproductive to communication. Layering questions is a skill that must be mastered through practice and appropriate application. Try it tonight when your get home. Ask a member of your family, "How was your day?"

"Fine."

"Tell me more about it."

"Oh, blah, blah, blah."

"What else?"

"Well, then blah, blah, blah."

"Go on."

Now you're in deep. Good news or bad, you're going to get to know what's really happening in that person's life. If the person is important to you, make the conversation important and get to the heart of the matter.

TWO COMMUNICATION CRIMES

The art of communication involves asking and layering great questions and listening with the intent to truly understand the other person. That being said, I urge you to avoid two common communication crimes that many salespeople (especially men) are uniquely guilty of committing.

The first one is fixing things. Upon hearing your prospects' objectives, challenges, or problems, the tendency is to jump in and present how your product, service, or program can help. There is a time and place for presenting your solutions, but now, in the discovery process, is neither the time nor the place. Right now you have your prospects in therapy. It's their turn. It's the thoughts inside their heads we're after, not yours.

The second communication crime is to heap technique upon technique. Don't use leftover techniques from the 1970s like repeating your prospects' answers, or "parroting," and asking lame questions such as, "Is that important to you?" Also forget about "mirroring," or mimicking your prospects' posture or gestures. These are all tricks that prospects see coming a mile away. These sales-psychobabble techniques are tired and in desperate need of being replaced with simple, sincere, human communication.

LEADING THE WITNESS

When I was going to management school, I took some law classes and learned a thing or two about how trial attorneys communicate, much of which applies to sales. One of my assignments included attending trials and observing attorneys in action, paying special attention to a particular trial technique. One such assignment was to observe how attorneys *"lead their witnesses,"* or put words in their mouths, through a line of questioning that flushes out the desired information and persuades the jury to reach the desired conclusion.

Leading the witness involves asking questions that suggest the answer within them. For example, "Wouldn't it be true that _____?" This is obviously a closed-ended question that requires a yes or no answer. Now, how does this apply in sales and the discovery process?

Sometimes, in the discovery process, you'll encounter prospects who are single-minded in their objectives, pre-occupied, just don't feel like thinking about your questions, or stay on the first level even after being prompted with layered questions. Classic examples are the CFO who is stuck on reducing costs, the department manager who just can't get beyond the challenge of "introducing any change into the workplace," or the purchasing agent who is focused only on getting the best price. Some people just can't seem to get off their only top-of-mind pet goals or issues without a little help.

A good trial attorney would lead this prospect by saying, "When I work with other CFOs, I often find that another objective they have is to _____. Would that be true for you?" Or you could say, "Many CFOs are constantly looking for ways to _____. Would that be an additional objective of yours?" For the single-minded office manager, you could try, "I notice that beyond introducing anything new into the workplace, another challenge facing office managers is _____. Is that a challenge that you share?" Or, to that stubborn purchasing agent fixed on price, you could ask, "Besides price, some purchasing departments are looking for ways to consolidate vendors. Is this something you would like to do?"

When asking consultative questions, it's a good idea to have a few answers ready in case your prospect looks like a deer in headlights. Having two or three additional objectives, challenges, or common issues puts you in a position to *suggest* fresh options and get prospects thinking outside their boxes. The more information you have—objectives, challenges, and issues, the more possibilities open up for positioning yourself, your product, service, or programs as the way to help your prospects achieve their goals and overcome their challenges.

Be prepared with a list of great consultative and discovery questions. Become skilled at articulating and layering your questions and formally documenting your prospects' responses. Also, be prepared to lead your prospects even deeper into their subconscious thoughts in order to flush out the critical information that is individual to them, their organizations, their departments, their jobs.

THE MOST PREDICTABLE DISCONNECTS IN SALES

Here you are at the fourth step in the *PowerSelling* consultative sales process. You've used your prospecting approach to create a selling opportunity, done some pre-call investigation to prepare for the first sales call, gone in and built executive-level rapport over a cup of coffee, and now your discovery step is nearly complete.

Some sales professionals may be able to conduct their full discovery during one call with only one contact. For others, it may take a sequence of calls, days of "wandering around," and developing relationships with multiple sources and contacts deep and wide within the account.

The next step, then, in the conventional sales process, is to translate your discovery findings into specifications, a scope of services, product offerings, and a proposal. Normally, the next appointment with the prospect is a presentation of your company's value proposition and service capabilities, perhaps a demonstration or trial of your product, and a then the delivery of your proposal, after which you attempt to gain commitment and close the sale.

Here is where I find the most likely and predictable *"disconnect"* in the conventional sales process. Prospects either accept your ideas and proposal with a few minor objections, or they say something like, "This looks fine to me. I'll get back to you in a few days or weeks." This is what I refer to as "being put into *orbit.*" Prospects launch you just beyond their gravitational pull, leaving you to circle around aimlessly like a satellite, lost in space. Most salespeople are then destined to make relentless follow-up calls that go something like this, "I'm calling to see if you need any more information to make a decision," or "I'm just calling to follow-up on my proposal and see where you are in your decision process." This kind of follow-up can go on indefinitely. All the while, your prospect is in total control of the entire process, the time frame, your sale, and your psyche.

The second-most-predictable disconnect in the conventional sales process occurs when prospects are blunt with you and flat out reject your proposal altogether. Their answer is "No, your recommendations or financial offer is not acceptable." Now, late in the sales process, you find yourself playing defense.

In this defensive position, many salespeople retreat to their offices to rethink their strategies and redesign their proposals. In the meantime, the prospect gets frustrated and either goes shopping for other ideas, offers, and terms, or decides not to decide. In either case, a frustrating impasse occurs for both the buyer and the seller. The relentless follow-up begins and looks like a tennis match for days to weeks, both sides volleying new offers, counteroffers, objections, responses, and more elaborate disconnects.

The Executive Summary: The Consultative Deliverable

What I am going to share with you now is the most profound sales tool I've ever discovered. I've personally used this tool to build my consulting business, and I've trained thousands of salespeople who have experienced dramatic results in closing sales when they implement this idea. It is the single-most-effective way to get prospects engaged in the sales process and be a part of designing their own proposal, which leads to their acceptance the proposal more than 80 percent of the time!

A LITTLE BACKGROUND

As I mentioned earlier, in my research on building a consulting business, I discovered the discouraging statistic that 90 percent of consultants go out of business in their first year, and another 5 percent go out of business in their second year. A 95 percent failure rate. Great!

Not to be discouraged by a little challenge, I decided to seek out some professional advice on the consulting business. I found several seminars offered by high-powered consultants who were willing, for some fat fees, to share their secrets, methods, and strategies with new entrepreneurs like me. In these conferences, I learned the traditional consulting process of analyze, design, implement, and measure. I learned how to conduct a consultative discovery process, profile accounts by documenting my discovery findings, target areas in which my innovations could deliver the most immediate results, and, as an outsider, build multiple relationships within a client's organization.

THE MISSING LINK

It was in one of these conferences that I was exposed to the consultant's secret weapon, "the deliverable," or what I refer to in this book as the *Executive Summary*. The Executive Summary is a step in the consulting process that is the ultimate solution to the two most common "disconnects" in the conventional sales process. It is the missing link that ties the consultant's discovery process to the proposal. When I first saw this step and this tool presented in the consulting process, I knew immediately that, if it were incorporated into the sales process, the Executive Summary would revolutionize consultative selling.

When inserted into the sales process, the Executive Summary creates an opportunity for prospects to collaborate with the salesperson as a consultant. Through this consultative and collaborative process, you can determine what recommendations you should propose, how you should construct the proposal, and how you should implement the recommendations. It's a pre-proposal that provides prospects an opportunity to participate in the design of their own final proposals. This tool also supports salespeople in the art of collaboration, which transforms prospects into advocates and creates enormous competitive distinction.

In a strict sense, the Executive Summary is a formal report of your discovery findings. It documents your prospect's objectives, challenges, and impacts. It offers a snapshot of your prospect's current methods and costs and identifies areas in which improvements can be made. It also contains your preliminary recommendations and innovative methods that will deliver solutions to your prospect's problems.

The Executive Summary compares and contrasts your prospect's current methods and costs with the proposed methods and costs of your recommendations. It is not a full-blown proposal yet, but a summary. At the end of the Executive Summary is an Implementation Agenda that describes the proposed action steps that both organizations—buyers and sellers—will need to take in order to successfully implement the recommendations. Each action step has a proposed date assigned to it that helps you *"open the closing conversation"* and prevent disconnects.

Here is a highly effective format for crafting a consultative Executive Summary:

- Top-level and Mid-level Management Objectives/ Challenges/Impacts

- Findings—a report of the current situation and methods

- Cost Analysis—current operating costs

- Areas for Improvement—problems with current methods

- Recommendation of Solutions—proposed new methods

- Benefits Summary—list of benefits your solutions deliver

- Implementation Agenda

Your Executive Summary doesn't need to be a novel. Keep it a true summary, an overview. I've seen simple two-page letters that clearly and concisely restate a prospect's current situation, offer initial recommendations, and propose action items and dates for implementation. Depending on the scope of discovery, I've also seen salespeople invest fifty to eighty hours writing hundred-page executive summaries that clearly demonstrate their deep understanding of the prospect's business environment, vision, preferences, and applications. I've also witnessed the enormous credibility earned by salespeople who package and present their recommendations into a legacy report that both educates prospects and offers insights that help them be better decision makers.

Once you've established the format for your consultative Executive Summary, you can, to some extent, automate the process, to accelerate the report writing. Here are a few principles for successfully crafting and presenting your Executive Summary:

Keep It Customized to the Prospect

Avoid the temptation of templates. Cutting and pasting in objectives, challenges, and problem areas from another prospect's report as filler will only dilute the effectiveness and credibility of your report.

Avoid Assumptions or Using Industry Averages

To gain even more credibility, use real-world data that are exclusive to your prospect's individual environment. By using actual numbers related to your prospect's operating costs, yields, volumes, etc., your reports will offer unique data that will help you and your prospect arrive at better decisions. If and when you do resort to using "industry averages," always get the prospect's agreement beforehand. You don't need surprise challenges during your presentation of the findings.

Be Prepared to Write Commentary

This is nonnegotiable! You must be willing to invest the effort and be skilled in structuring sentences, crafting paragraphs, and compiling pages of commentary in order to provide full value to your prospect and create true competitive distinction. I know this hurts! Most great salespeople I know aren't great writers. However, this is how executive reports are developed and delivered. Avoid using simple bullet points that list only three or four loosely related words. Bullet points are for PowerPoint presentations where the presenter can embellish these points and abbreviated phrases. Using bullet points exposes you to the risk of prospects making their own interpretations, or having to work too hard to decipher the information. This can lead to frustration with, and shelving of, the document. If necessary, get help from a professional writer.

Create Rough Drafts

Never, never, never sit down to your computer to write an Executive Summary the day before you have to present it to a prospect. First, sit down with your discovery findings, all of your interview notes, all the cost data you've collected, and all other related information, and just wallow in the information for a while as you sip some coffee.

Explore the information with the intent of identifying those objectives and challenges that should be priorities, problems that are most pressing, and costs that are out of control. Begin to develop your general recommendations. Jot down your thoughts within your defined format without limiting your creative process by having to get it perfect the first time. Go back later and rewrite another draft with more specific commentary. Go through this fine-tuning process two or three times, adding some polish to each draft until you're ready to key in your report. Something magic happens in the process of working through the various rough drafts. The more you handle the information, the more you internalize the information. When it comes time to present the Executive Summary, you'll surprise yourself at your command of the information and how you are able to present with more conviction and passion.

Proofread the Entire Draft

I know this is elementary, but I am often amazed at the horrific sales letters and proposals I see being delivered to executives. Ask yourself, "What level of education does my prospect have?" If you're delivering your summary to a CFO, vice president of finance, or a vice president of human resources, your prospects will most likely have advanced degrees or even MBAs. At the very least, they will have undergraduate degrees and be well-read individuals. They most certainly will notice if sentences are not properly structured or if words are misspelled or misused.

I suggest that you proofread your Executive Summary out loud to yourself. Yes, out loud! It's here that you will *hear mistakes* that you won't catch simply by reading silently. Next, give your report to a third party to proofread. By this time, you will be too close to the information to be objective and fully critical of your own writing. Have someone else provide input on clarity and validate context and grammar. You'll be amazed at how helpful it is to have another set of eyes and ears contribute to the project. The outcome is that with every draft, edit, and proofread, you end up with a better-quality deliverable.

Rehearse the Presentation

Before you grab your Executive Summary from the binding machine and race to your presentation, stop for a few moments and practice your delivery. It's best if you can present it to someone who can listen objectively and lend some constructive criticism. Put forth this extra effort and you'll amaze yourself at your smooth delivery, resulting in predictable effectiveness.

THE SECRETS OF POWERSELLING: CONSULTING & COLLABORATING

So here you are. You've conducted a comprehensive discovery, you've documented your findings in your Executive Summary, provided a complete description of the prospect's current situation and written commentary on the problem areas. For every problem, your Executive Summary offers a recommended solution. Your recommendations explain where and how your expertise, products, and services will help the prospect meet objectives, eliminate challenges, and solve problems.

Now you're ready. You know more about the prospect's business, relative to your area of expertise, than the prospect does, and then some. You've internalized this information, practiced your delivery, and know that your recommendations are sound. You know exactly where to target your efforts and resources to yield the quickest, highest-impact results. Now you're ready to present your Executive Summary to the prospect. You'll find that the next two steps are simply brilliant!

CONSULTING: PRESENTING THE EXECUTIVE SUMMARY

Let's talk about the nuances of presenting your Executive Summary. Again, these suggestions are based on personal experience and feedback from hundreds of eagles I've interviewed who have had extraordinary results with this tool.

First, before you jump into your glossy report, stop and think for a minute. This is just like any other sales call, so how do you start? Right, first you build rapport with the prospect. Have a cup of coffee and migrate into the presentation once the two of you are connected as people, talking some business.

Once you're both comfortable, it's critical that you briefly review your discovery process. Bring out some of your supporting evidence—interview notes, cost information, and critical data you've collected—to validate the significant work and time you've put into this process. Explain how and from what sources within the prospect's organization you collected the data.

Describe your site survey and your discovery interviews with mid-level management. This is not to win effort points. This validation of your process lends credibility to your summary and on many occasions short circuits any challenges to your findings that the prospect may bring up during your presentation. Be prepared. You may have to refer to your supporting evidence if your information is challenged.

Now simply begin presenting the findings in your Executive Summary, starting with the statement of top management's objectives, challenges, and impacts. Gain validation along the way and get your prospect engaged in and comfortable with participating in this discussion.

Your Executive Summary should contain a quick "snapshot" page that summarizes the prospect's current situation. This snapshot may be a quantitative overview that shows the prospect's current methods and accumulative costs. Review the current situation, pointing out any areas of concern or opportunities that jump off the page. This may include areas where current methods are not sufficient or where costs are seriously out of control, either case begging for further inspection and consideration.

Now comes the tricky part. Most high-level executives like to know what and where their problem areas are. Their thinking is that if they know what needs fixing, they can fix it. For mid-level managers, however, this can be a sensitive subject; they feel that the disclosure of problems may reflect poorly on their ability to manage. If mid-level managers are present at your presentation, be careful here.

I always open the discussion of problem areas by explaining that I am trained to look for problems in my area of expertise that may not be obvious to most people. I also explain that ten out of ten times I conduct a site survey, I find that even the best organizations have business processes that can be improved. I am now at the point where I can successfully engage in the strategy of *collaborative prioritization* and set the stage for a pre-approved proposal.

Sample
Executive Summary
For the Document Technology Industry

Executive

Summary

For

GlobalOne

Agenda

- ✓ Objectives & Challenges in Producing & Managing Documents at GlobalOne
- ✓ Findings
- ✓ Total Volume and Cost Analysis Charts
- ✓ Cost Analysis By Technology Charts
- ✓ Areas for Improvement
- ✓ Suggested Implementation Plan
- ✓ Proposed Implementation Schedule
- ✓ Output Technology Analysis

Objectives & Challenges in Producing & Managing Documents at GlobalOne

Objectives

It was determined that the objectives in producing and managing documents at GlobalOne are:

- To better understand our document environment and related technology. To analyze all document technologies in place, such as copiers, printers, facsimiles, color printers, jobs outsourced and related human interaction, operating costs, vendor obligations, and volumes.

  Based on a clear understanding of the enterprise-wide document management and print environment, GlobalOne can go on to develop an effective print-management strategy which will increase workflow productivity while reducing operating expenses.

- To create internal and external communication via "documents on demand." To route the right information to the right people at the right time and in the right format. "To inventory the least amount of documents possible and reduce the number of devices." To utilize our network to better create, manage, transport, and output documents; improving our return on investment.

- To control and minimize the cost associated with reproducting and distributing documents.
  "To identify our total cost of ownership and areas where costs are out of control."
  GlobalOne is currently charged with the mandate to examine all line-item expenditures with the outcome of reducing operating costs by 12-15% by Q2.

- To support human resources with technology that will enable them to get their work done with fewer interruptions, while increasing department workflow productivity and the quality of documents. In the legal department, "We need to consider replacing user-intensive, manual filing and retrieval of hard copy documents to a simplified image capture, archive, and retrieval system."

- To streamline the number of vendors providing document delivery systems. "The main objective here is to achieve consistency in pricing, programs, invoicing, and support for our document production."

Objectives & Challenges in Producing & Managing Documents at GlobalOne

Challenges

It was determined that the biggest challenges facing GlobalOne in the area of document production and management are:

- ◆ GlobalOne has redundancy in technology, consumables, office space, operating costs, human steps, and waste related to documents, which "lowers productivity and distracts from the bottom line."

- ◆ GlobalOne has eight vendors associated with the production of documents. Managing this variety of vendors is time-intensive and expensive. Vendors for software, hardware, service, and supplies have their own invoices, contracts, personnel, and policies, which encourages finger pointing among vendors and creates lack of accountability.

- ◆ Down time anywhere in the document-flow process impacts the next stage, holding up people and workflow in other departments. Down time in the process creates frustration among human resources because it places unnecessary urgency to meet unreasonable deadlines.

- ◆ The lack of standardization of output technology leads to end-user confusion (help desk calls), training issues, the need to inventory multiple toner cartridges in work groups, and "people walking to locate devices which offer the features they need to get their work done." Some older legacy devices are under utilized, while newer more feature-rich devices are being over utilized. This leads to lines at the devices, downtime due to overburdened usage, and cost-recovery challenges.

- ◆ The current document technology is not integrated, forcing users to walk from their printers to a copier and then sometimes to the fax machine in order to produce and distribute documents. This action is repeated numerous times a day, decreasing personal productivity and increasing the cost of documents.

Findings

GlobalOne has the following document technology, related monthly volumes, and costs:

Technology	# Units	Monthly Vol	# Invoices	Monthly Cost	Cost Per Page
Copiers	8	152,310	5.98	$4,297.11	0.0282
Printers	22	123,213	7.21	$3,623.76	0.0294
Facsimiles	6	6,500	0.96	$784.60	0.1207
Color Imaging Systems	2	7,316	1.00	$916.33	0.1253
Mainframe Printing	1	36,000	0.00	$1,673.00	0.0465
	39	**325,339**	**15.15**	**$11,294.80**	**0.0347**

Related costs consist of the following:

Related Cost	Included In Totals Above (Device Related)	Non-Device Related
Labor	$0.00	$10,632.00
Facsimiles-Long Distance Charges	$199.00	$0.00
	$199.00	**$10,632.00**

Outsourced documents consist of the following:

	Color Imaging	Long Runs	Processing and Assembly	TOTALS
# Jobs	2	2	2	6
Monthly Vol	2,000	151,610	560	154,170
# Invoices	1.00	1.00	1.00	3.00
Monthly Cost	$2,757.00	$5,350.00	$319.00	$8,426.00
Cost Per Page	$1.3785	$0.0353	$0.5696	$0.0547

Total Combined Document Volume : 479,509 Pages Per Month

Total Monthly Document Production Costs : $30,352.80

Total # of Vendors : 5

Total # of Invoices Processed : 18.15 at a Cost of $60.00 Each

For a Total Invoice Processing Cost of $1,089.00 Per Month

Overall Total Cost Per Page : $0.0633

Areas for Improvement

Enterprise

Facsimiles

Fax machines are shared by many employees, so often the fax is busy or there is a line of people waiting to use it.

90% of fax jobs are twelve pages or less and required two to three times per day. The turnaround time for the typical fax job is five minutes. Users spend an average of fifteen minutes per day at the fax machine.

Document Production

Most documents at GlobalOne begin in a digital format, either entered or scanned onto the system at a work station. Most every work group has a scanner, printer, copier, and a fax in order to create, duplicate, and distribute documents.

Each of these devices represents six elements:
1) Capital expenditure
2) Operating cost (service, consumables, power consumption)
3) Office space
4) Human involvement (walking and waiting, loading toner & paper)
5) Deterioration in quality (printer = 1200 DPI, copier = 600 DPI, fax = 300 DPI)
6) Vendor administration (presentations, contracts, invoices, account reviews)

Typically each person prints original documents to the printer, then walks to the copier to produce sets, then walks to the fax, and then to the mail room to distribute the documents to a remote location.

This fragmented mix of legacy technology and the related human steps in processing documents results in low personal productivity, high operating costs, high consumption of space, power, and administration time.

Areas for Improvement

Administration

Network Printers

The existing printers produce ten to sixteen pages per minute and offer no personal productivity features, such as collating or finishing. The average turnaround time for each set of documents is twelve minutes plus, collating time. This represents 1.2 hours per day per assistant, or 105.6 hour per month for the department, just to print documents.

Copying Systems

Typical print jobs in Administration are printed to the printer and then walked to a copier to produce six sets for the executive committee. The normal report in this department is five to ten pages run several times per day.

The average turnaround time for the average job is twelve minutes when there is no line at the copier. (fifteen to twenty minutes if the copier is in use as a user has to walk to locate another device.)

If the average user requires the average job five to ten times per day this equates to a minimum of two hours per day that end-users are walking originals from printers to copiers and waiting for documents. This totals forty-four to sixty-six hours per month per user! (twenty-two working days per month)

Facsimiles

Administration produces daily sales stats for each sales manager which are distributed via fax each day. The average report is twelve pages and takes four minutes to fax which represents forty-four minutes per day or 16.3 hours per month.

Nine of the managers require long distance connections which cost $197 per month. Also, receiving the report via fax cost seven cents per page or $19 per month, per branch or $209.

Areas for Improvement

Administration

Mainframe Printing

Administration frequently produces large enterprise reports, including inventory reports, registers, journals, and SKU reports. Many of these reports are seventy-five plus pages with five sets produced onto 11 X 15 green bar paper. The average monthly cost for production of these reports is $1,088.

Administration also prints GlobalOne's invoices from their AS400 system onto pre-printed, multi-part invoice forms. The monthly cost for invoice production is $600.

Filing

The Administration department is considering an initiative to go paperless, starting with current documents and then scanning in historical documents to replace hard copy file cabinets. The outcome is to reduce time required locating files in storage, retrieving and copying files, and then replacing the originals back into storage (office space).

Combined, the administrative assistants spend an average of forty-four hours per month searching for historical documents at a cost of $29 per hour, or $1,276 per month.

Training

Network Printers

The printers in this department are over utilized in both monthly volume and applications. Due to the volumes, print speeds, and lack of finishing features, these printers result in low productivity for the department.

Up to eight times per day, users print originals to the printer then walk them to the copier to make multiple sets, which are then sorted and stapled.

Turnaround time is up to fifteen minutes each time this job is required. This represents two hours per day per end-user or a total of six hours per day that end-users are producing documents at an output device.

Suggested Implementation Plan

General Comments

Facsimiles

By utilizing a combination of multifunctional devices and lan fax software, work groups can eliminate the high cost of faxing documents while increasing personal productivity by sending and receiving faxes from their desktops.

With the proper end-user training, GlobalOne can reduce the walking and waiting (15 minutes per day, per person) to fax machines, increase personal productivity, lower operating costs, reduce the number of toner cartridges in work groups, save office space, and eliminate yet another vendor.

Enterprise Workgroups

The implementation of multifunctional technology (scan, print, copy, fax, & e-mail from the desktop) will reduce GlobalOne personnel from walking and waiting from device to device, multiple toner cartridges in the work group, vendor administration, operating costs, long-distance costs, consumption of power and office space and result in higher quality documents.

The implementation of MFT devices will also result in cost savings via consolidation of capital expenditures, operating costs, and related costs (human steps).

Total Office Systems has targeted work groups with intensive document production applications with high volumes and operating costs and will recommend specific multifunctional technology according the specific applications of that department. The recommendations will guarantee increased work group productivity while reducing operating costs via consolidation.

Suggested Implementation Plan

Administration

Network Printers

By installing multifunctional technology (scan, print, copy) in this department, documents can be produced in original print quality from one device that offers 300% faster print speed plus finishing features such as collation and stapling.

With this new technology, the average job turnaround time for will go from twelve minutes, plus human collating time, to four minutes including collating time. Document production time in this department will go from over 105 hours per month ($3,045) to 35 hours per month ($1,015).

Mainframe Printing

For the large, enterprise reports produced on expensive green bar paper and invoices, we recommend a high-speed, high-volume production solution with AS 400 output management software, which will eliminate the need for green bar paper, pre-printed multi-part forms, and the impact printer.

This approach will guarantee increased workflow productivity and reliability in this critical environment. With suites of hardware and software technology solutions, you can also capture, merge, and route print output from the AS/400 to a variety of output devices, including laser printers, multifunctional systems, fax systems, e-mail systems, and file archives.

This suite of solutions will increase flexibility in the types of paper and font choices available for reporting. It will also provide automated finishing functionality, duplexing which reduces paper consumption, and document format modification.

A significant savings can be created in this department in the reduction of supply costs plus related costs of labor-intensive processes such as loading, bursting, stripping, collating, and distributing reports and invoices.

121

Proposed Implementation Schedule

➡ 4/12/04   Total Office Systems and GlobalOne prioritize suggested solutions for implementation and agree on date for delivery of proposal.

➡ 4/15/04   Total Office Systems and GlobalOne review the proposal for prioritized solutons with the outcome of arriving at an implementation decision.

➡ 4/15/04   Total Office Systems and GlobalOne finalize documentation:
* Purchase Order
* Lease Documents
* Credit Application

➡ 4/19/04   Total Office System's technical staff conducts pre-installation site survey to confirm:
* Space and power requirements
* Network compatibility
* Installation logistics

➡ 4/21/04   Total Office Systems installs systems and conducts intial key-operator and end-user training.

➡ Ongoing   Total Office Systems conducts training as necessary to assure the maximization of value of GlobalOne's information delivery system.

➡ Semi-Annually   Account Reviews will be conducted to measure the results of these recommendations, analyze ongoing cost of ownership, and determine further opportunities to innovate document production at GlobalOne.

CHAPTER 8

Collaborating & Prioritizing to Design the Pre-Approved Proposal

A t this point in the presentation of the Executive Summary, I simply tell the prospect, "As your consultant, I'm going to review all the problem areas I've identified and offer a recommendation for each one. But as your consultant, I would never dream of implementing all of these recommendations at once. As we discuss the areas for improvement and the solutions, I recommend that you and I *work together* to focus on the top three to four areas you see as *priorities."*

I guarantee that if you leave out this set-up, you'll get halfway through the problem areas and hit a wall. Your prospect will become defensive, get tangled in the details, and become preoccupied with the now seemingly overwhelming scope of work.

If you were thorough in your discovery, you may have identified several problems and have a wide scope of recommendations. Let's say, for example, that you've documented twelve to fifteen problem areas and thus have twelve to fifteen recommended solutions, each containing an element or combination of products or services that will need to be included in your subsequent proposal.

Here's the obvious question. What normally happens when you charge in with a proposal that is wide in scope, requiring prospects to drastically change the way they operate? Furthermore, because your proposal is wide in scope, it reaches a relatively high financial threshold. What normally happens to huge proposals?

Usually, when too much change is suggested too fast, too much money is on the line, and too much commitment to one new vendor is involved, the prospect will get spooked and do one or all of the following: build up a resistance to change, get more people involved in the decision, start to comparison shop, and, at the very least, invite the incumbent vendor in for a quotation. The result is that you've done a lot of work for nothing. Here, in the *PowerSelling* process, is where some brilliant strategy and a little patience pay off handsomely.

The strategy is to get your prospect to participate in *prioritizing your recommendations* and become involved in implementing your solutions before you even deliver your proposal. By collaborating with your prospects to identify which of your recommendations *they* want to implement first (prioritization), thus which of your recommendations they want proposed, you exponentially improve your chances of having your proposal accepted.

By prioritizing your recommendations, you will, in effect, "right-size" your scope of work and your related proposal to a digestible chunk. This will most likely ensure that the prospect approves your proposal without getting more people involved in the decision or waking up the incumbent vendor.

In consulting we call this *"phasing in the solutions."* Phase one is to implement the top three to four solutions over a reasonable time frame and measure the results. Phase two, upon confirmation of results, or earning the right, is to implement the next three or four prioritized solutions, and so on, until all the solutions are implemented over time.

Phasing in the solutions gives the prospect a chance to

implement manageable projects without assuming the huge risk associated with introducing drastic changes, totally changing vendors, and committing huge financial resources all at once. This process also helps you initially implement a manageable scope of work and deliver quick results. This leads to greater credibility, trust, and acceptance in implementing subsequent phases.

As you continue to go through your presentation, engage your prospect in discussing your findings, asking which of the problems are critical, or *"must solve now,"* which would classify as *"solve in phase two,"* and which fall in the category of *"solve in phase three,"* and so on.

Also engage your prospect in discussing how you will work together to implement the solutions. If applicable, explain how you and your support team will work with the prospect's management team to implement the solutions.

Now you've demonstrated your consultative and collaborative sales process and proven your expertise in designing innovative solutions. Your prospect agrees that there are problem areas and have chosen which ones to solve.

Once you've reviewed your recommended solutions, revisit the prioritization list. Suggest that, based on this collaboration, you will offer a proposal on the *top-priority* solutions with the idea of *"getting started"* and *"earning the right"* to be the prospect's solution provider on an ongoing basis.

This is where patience comes into the picture. If you embrace this consultative process, you must be prepared to scale down your initial scope of work and your initial proposal to the top three to four priorities, get those solutions implemented, measure your effectiveness (results), and return every ninety to 120 days to review your results and then prioritize the next three to four recommendations.

In a way, your Executive Summary acts as a proposal for the proposal. It sets you up for presenting a final proposal that hits the target spot-on. It gets prospects engaged and committed to owning their problems and solving their problems with your solutions. It truly is the secret weapon of *PowerSelling*. But there is still one more element of the Executive Summary that adds a turbocharged effect to the whole process.

OPENING THE CLOSING CONVERSATION: THE IMPLEMENTATION AGENDA

When a new client engages me, it's very common that top management requests that I teach its salespeople how to close sales more effectively. I love it when management and salespeople show up expecting some kind of magic pill or revolutionary new closing technique that will help them "get the ink on the paper."

Many salespeople view closing as a climactic event, the finale to a grand scheme. When it comes to closing, however, I believe in the time-tested adage, *"Close early and close often"* — that is, close the sale multiple times along the way. In addition to trial closes throughout the sales process, sales eagles have used the simple *Implementation Agenda* for decades as a way to *open the closing conversation* well before showing up with contracts.

Traditionally, most salespeople use the Implementation Agenda as the last page of their proposal. In the *PowerSelling* model, I've moved it to the last page of the Executive Summary. By presenting it here, before the proposal is delivered, you create an opportunity to *future pace* your prospect. The Implementation Agenda allows you to collaborate with the prospect on the logistical process for implementing your solutions. It also helps you open the discussion as to how and when you intend to close the sale.

On your Implementation Agenda, simply list the steps both organizations—buyer and seller—will need to take to successfully implement your solutions. By identifying the steps in sequence and attaching realistic time frames for each, you are pacing your prospect through future events that will lead to the sale.

The first step is the review of the Executive Summary. The date attached is obviously the date you present your Executive Summary to the prospect. The next step is for you and your prospect to prioritize the solutions your prospect wants to implement. The date attached is the same as your Executive Summary presentation date. The next step is the presentation of your proposal for the products and services encompassed in your prioritized solutions. The date attached is ideally within a few days of the presentation of the Executive Summary. The next step listed is that your prospect must approve the proposal. Just to make things interesting, attach the same date as the presentation of your proposal.

Both organizations must then "complete documentation," that is, the prospect must generate a purchase order, cut a deposit check, sign contracts, provide credit applications, and complete whatever paperwork is required to conclude the transaction. Again, to keep it interesting, attach the same date as the presentation and approval of the proposal.

The last few steps are yours. List the steps your organization must take in order to successfully implement the solutions; fulfill the agreement; and provide the products, services, training, etc. The dates attached to these steps are in relationship to the scope of work and your agreement with the customer. The final action items on your Implementation Agenda should reflect your commitment to provide follow-up, conduct account reviews, and assure total customer satisfaction on an ongoing basis.

"CONFRONTATION ACCELERATES EITHER SUCCESS OR FAILURE"

Let's go back to *opening the closing conversation*. The first few action steps and dates should be easily agreed on by both the buyer and seller. For example, prioritizing the recommendations and then reviewing the proposal for those solutions should present no push-back from the prospect. Remember that the next step is for the prospect to approve the proposal, and that the date you've attached is the same date as your presentation of the proposal.

In reviewing your Implementation Agenda, here's where a perfect world usually becomes the real world, and that's what you want. You want to know where you stand, what the prospect is thinking, the probability of closing the sale, and a realistic time frame for closing the sale.

If you're going to get a push-back or stall at closing time, let's find out beforehand what it's going to be, why, how long, and what needs to happen in order to get a favorable decision. In a way, you're inviting a push-back, an objection, or at least asking for a further education as to how your prospect makes decisions and conducts business. Here's where your prospect may say, "I can review your proposal next Tuesday, but I'm not in a position to approve it at that time." So far your goal has been accomplished—you've opened the closing conversation.

It's up to you to simply ask the prospect what needs to happen in order to approve the proposal. Get it out on the table now, before you even propose! You may hear anything from "I need to run this by my executive committee or accountant," to "It's our policy to send out Request for Proposals for these types of acquisitions."

Engage your prospect in discussing the specifics of this internal decision-making process and garner input as to a realistic time frame for implementation. During this conversation, you can modify the Implementation Agenda, adding action steps and reassigning dates until you've arrived at an agreement that works for both you and the prospect. By discussing the required steps for concluding the transaction, you've engaged your prospect in a highly collaborative closing conversation.

I know some salespeople who successfully present their Implementation Agendas with the dates left blank. They engage their prospects right from the start, partnering with them, making requests of each other, offering proposals and counterproposals, and making commitments to each other's action steps, jointly deciding on realistic dates for completion. The outcome is to get prospects involved in and committed to closing the sale. Remember, all these closing action steps and dates are worked out and committed to before you even deliver your final proposal.

Before we move on, take a wild guess at the closing ratios my clients enjoy when they present a proposal for solutions that the prospect has already prioritized and pre-approved in principle. Keep in mind that they are presenting their proposals on agreed-upon dates, and that the prospect knows full well that the next action step is to approve the proposal on that same date. If you guessed around 80 percent, you're right!

CHAPTER 9

Propose Your Solutions and Present Your Value Proposition

W hen I visit sales organizations to conduct my discovery process, I ask to see the last ten proposals delivered to prospects. Many start out with an aimless cover letter that explains what's in the attached proposal. They rarely even bring up the desired end result—an agreement, a decision, a sale.

After the cover letter, I often see that the content is not a proposal at all, but merely a *price quotation.* These proposals simply state product specifications or a description of services offered with a price attached. This is usually accompanied by a menu of the financing options and terms. Most every proposal I see incorporates some kind of value-building collateral to lend credibility. Usually, this value proposition material is in the *front* of the proposal package, and the pricing information is in the back of the document.

My point is, it's no wonder that so many salespeople tell me that closing sales in their industries gets down to the common denominator of a product/price comparison. I suggest that, based on the design of their proposals, these price quotations, many salespeople inadvertently drive their customers in that direction.

In this section I will share elements of winning proposals

that will accelerate getting favorable decisions from your prospects. Of course, these proposals will itemize product and service specifications, include pricing, and describe terms and conditions of the transaction as any proposal should. But instead of focusing on products, services, and pricing, we're going to stay the course and focus on *proposing solutions that help prospects meet their objectives*. We're then going to *cost justify* those solutions with a compelling proposal. I'll also introduce three investment justifications you can choose from that will ground your proposal in sound financial principles.

ELEMENTS OF THE WINNING PROPOSAL

Let's start with the cover letter. Begin by thanking the prospect for the opportunity to consult and collaborate together to get to this point. Next, simply restate what was decided upon in your last meeting. That includes reviewing the enclosed proposal to arrive at an approval for putting into motion the steps for implementing the solutions.

Go on to provide an overview of the proposal's content. Briefly list what's included. For example, a description of your solutions, product specifications, scope of work for services, cost justification, your value proposition, contract terms, and samples of related documentation. That's right, documentation. Any proposal should include the actual or sample documents required to move forward and formalize the agreement. This may include a letter of intent, an application, contract, or even a checklist detailing all the documentation required.

Close your cover letter by reminding the prospect that you are there to present solutions, review the financial offer, and discuss the *final logistics of implementing those solutions*. Future pace the prospect by saying that you're looking forward to a favorable decision and a mutually productive, long-term relationship.

Next, before you jump into product specifications or a description of services, take a small step back and remain consistent with the consultative process. In the first section of your proposal, titled *"Objectives & Challenges,"* briefly restate the prospect's primary objectives and challenges that your proposal will address.

The second section of the proposal may be titled, *"Solutions, Specifications and Support."* Introduce your specific solutions, products, and services in detail. Include specifications, descriptions of your support and customer service programs, guarantees, warranties, installation, training services, etc. It is in this section that you will present your financial options as well. Here, it is up to you to package your financial offer in a way that is appropriate for your products or services. You will itemize your acquisition options, financing terms, fee-based a la carte options, and the terms of your proposal. You may also include a description of any value-added inclusions that you have bundled into your proposal.

Next is the *"Cost Analysis"* section. Cost analysis is easiest to present in a simple side-by-side format, but this is not mandatory. First, itemize your prospect's current situation and related costs on the left side of the page, then list your proposed itemized solutions and related costs on the right side. For both the prospect's current costs and your proposed costs, list all the elements of operating costs, or *total costs of ownership*. If your proposal includes some of these costs, make sure you indicate it here. For example, if your proposal includes customer support, itemize it and simply insert *"included"* in the space for this line item. I never use the words *"no charge"* or *"free,"* as they diminish the value of your inclusions.

At the conclusion of your side-by-side comparison, you have the opportunity to identify either an increase or decrease in total operating costs, or total costs of ownership. If your prospect expenses these costs monthly, then finish this section with a total monthly increase or decrease in expenses, which-ever is applicable.

If you are decreasing the prospect's expenses, thus saving money, then you will want to maximize that savings into an annual amount or even expand it over the life of the agreement. If you are increasing the prospect's expenses, then it's your job to *sell the difference* between what the prospect is currently paying and the proposed costs of your solutions. Selling the difference is sometimes as simple as listing the additional value and benefits the prospect receives for the additional outlay of costs. I'll offer more on this later in this chapter.

In more complex transactions, selling the difference is made easier with the next section of your proposal, which is titled, *"Investment Justification."* While there are entire books devoted to this topic, I will present a simplistic overview of three models that are proven to demonstrate, in black and white, how prospects can justify their investments, depending on their business model and financial applications.

PAYBACK, RETURN ON INVESTMENT, AND CASH-FLOW ANALYSIS

Sometimes life is good. For instance, there are some cases where your proposal saves the prospect money, generates revenues and related profits, or improves the prospect's cash-flow over time. For those who are fortunate enough to be in this position, the following are three powerful tools to include in a winning proposal. For justifying an investment that results in costs savings, consider providing your prospect with a payback/breakeven schedule. When your product will generate revenues, *or* substantial savings, you can use the Return on Investment (ROI) model. For long-term savings, I will present the Cash-Flow Analysis.

The Payback/Breakeven Model

My mortgage broker recently called and said I could re-finance my home for a flat fee of $5,000. I had just gone through this arduous process four months earlier and told him I didn't think it was worth the hassle. He quickly responded with the following logic:

By refinancing now at even a slightly lower interest rate, I could save $262 a month. But, to realize the savings, I had to put out $5,000 in fees. If I outlay $5,000 now to save $262 a month, the payback, or breakeven, is nineteen months. I not only get my $5,000 back in savings over the next nineteen months, but then I save $262 a month for the next 341 months. That's $89,342! How can I afford not to lay down the five grand?

The payback/breakeven model is simple and powerful. All you have to do is divide the initial investment amount ($5,000) by the monthly savings ($262) and voila, there's your payback, or breakeven, period. The payback/breakeven model is very effective for justifying investments and accelerating the decision-making process. If your prospects are going to get their initial investment back relatively soon in the form of savings, and then save more going forward on an ongoing basis, why would they wait?

Payback/Breakeven Formula:

$$\frac{\text{monthly or annual savings}}{\text{initial investment}} = \text{payback}$$

I witnessed another perfect example of the power of the payback/breakeven model while working with a salesperson in Amsterdam who was selling print-on-demand systems and related solutions. He was calling on a large firm with multiple locations. In his discovery process, he learned that the prospect was currently printing its payroll checks every week at the home office and distributing them to eleven branch offices throughout Europe via an overnight courier service. The cost of the courier service was approximately 200,000 euros per year.

The salesperson had innovative technology and solutions that enabled the prospect to distribute the payroll information over its existing network and print the checks on-demand at each of the eleven branches with complete security and accuracy. Now, the initial investment for the new print-on-demand technology was roughly 200,000 euros. In this case, the payback/breakeven is one year. Going forward, the customer saves 200,000 euros a year. This is a no-brainer for the client, and an easy road to a sale for the seller.

The Return on Investment Model

The pure application for the *Return on Investment* (ROI) model is when your product or service actually generates revenues and related profits for your client. For example, a computer workstation sold to a hotel business center generates rental revenues and profits. Jet skis sold to a resort marina generate rental revenues. An automobile fleet sold to a taxi company generates cab fares. Printers, copiers, and faxes sold to a law firm generate revenues and profits when the firm charges its clients for documents. I've also seen this model used to justify investments where the proposal generates significant cost savings for the prospect.

The pure ROI formula is fairly simple. First, you and your prospect must research and agree on the anticipated revenue and profit—the average, annual, net, pre-tax income (or costs savings)—that your product or service will generate over the life of the project or agreement. Next, divide that amount by the total investment over the life of the project. This will give you your return on investment in a percentage figure. Here's the formula and an example:

Return on Investment Formula:

$$\frac{\text{average annual net pre-tax income or costs savings}}{\text{cost of proposed investment (project costs)}} = \text{ROI percentage}$$

Return on Investment Example:

$$\frac{\$36,000 \text{ average annual net pre-tax income}}{\$65,000 \text{ investment over 3 years}} = 55\% \text{ ROI}$$

In the example above, the resort marina is paying $65,000 for jet skis over a three-year life span. In those three years, it anticipates generating $36,000 in profits, yielding a 55 percent return on its investment. That's a stellar ROI when compared to placing that same $65,000 in a sail boat, where it may only achieve a 15 percent ROI, or even a CD at the bank, which generates a mere 3 to 5 percent ROI per year. Even over three years, that's only a 15 percent ROI, versus 55 percent.

Many companies have policies that require them to justify every investment with the application of an ROI formula. Many will set the minimum ROI they expect before they'll approve any transaction. It's a good idea to inquire early if this is the case and then collaborate with your prospect on the incorporation of this tool in your proposal.

Cash-Flow Analysis

For larger investments with long life cycles, I have never seen a more powerful tool for justifying the investment and accelerating the decision process than cash-flow analysis.

The best-suited environment is where the buyer is currently using assets, such as equipment or technology *that will need to be replaced within a reasonable time frame, at a substantial investment.* This model assumes that your proposal will result in reduced total cost of ownership over the prospect's current costs. For example, let's look at a prospect who will replace its telecommunications systems within the next five years at a cost of $1 million.

To accelerate the decision-making process and lessen the financial impact of the million-dollar investment, the salesperson must demonstrate that, over the next five years, the prospect will spend substantially more money supporting and ultimately replacing its current system than if it replaces it now with new technology *at a reduced operating cost.* Let's say the prospect is currently spending $125,000 per year maintaining the existing system (operating costs) and your new system will reduce that operating costs to just $25,000 per year. That's an annual savings of $100,000.

Example: Existing telecom system with $1 million replacement cost in year three and annual operating costs of $125,000 per year.

Year 1	Year 2	Year 3	Year 4	Year 5	Total over 5 years
$125,000	$125,000	$1,125,000	$125,000	$125,000	= $1,625,000

New telecom system with $1 million replacement costs in year one and annual operating costs of $25,000 per year. (This is a $100,000 per year savings in operating cost for five years.)

Year 1	Year 2	Year 3	Year 4	Year 5	Total over 5 years
$1,025,000	$25,000	$25,000	$25,000	$25,000	= $1,125,000

Net savings = $500,000 over 5 years starting in year one.

In this example, your proposal begs the question, "Why wait?" If the prospect agrees that it will replace the existing telecom system in the next five years, that its existing operating costs will remain the same, and that your proposal will save over $8,000 per month effective immediately, why would the prospect wait even two or three months? Again, the power of this tool is to accelerate implementation of the savings, which will in turn accelerate the favorable decision.

I understand that I have presented a very simplistic overview of this relatively complex tool. There are accounting rules and assumptions that you must follow in order to implement this tool with credibility. If you think this cost justification tool applies to your sales model, I suggest that you seek out further consulting and training on the nuances of implementation.

I trust that, even after a very brief overview, you see the distinction between payback/breakeven, ROI, and cash-flow analysis in technical financial terms. Once you get some experience with the investment justification that suits your sales model, I guarantee you'll turbocharge your proposals and accelerate buying decisions.

A FEW MORE WORDS ON WINNING PROPOSALS

While I believe that cost analysis and investment justifications are the keys to winning proposals, there are nuances to these models that will help you use these tools most effectively.

First, it's critical to gain agreement from prospects as to what tangible and intangible elements motivate them in their financial decision-making process. Be sure to do this *prior* to the development and presentation of your proposal. You must determine if the prospects measure only tangible impacts on revenue and expenses — *hard costs and benefits* — or if they also measure intangibles such as improved quality, increased

productivity, or the ability to gain competitive distinction—
soft costs and benefits.

For example, if you're selling a law firm a digital document management system for $100,000 (hard costs), that's obviously a tangible impact on expenses. But let's go on to say that your technology will increase the personal productivity of every legal assistant by 35 percent while they cost the firm $50 per hour (soft costs). My question for you, and your question for your prospect, is, "Is this a tangible or intangible savings?" Another question is, "Should we build this savings into our investment justification?"

If your prospect considers the increased productivity of these legal assistants an intangible savings, you may want to provide a quick demonstration. Take two $50 bills from your wallet and put them on the table. Identify one of the bills as the burdened cost of the legal assistant, and one as the dollars invested in the solution you're selling. Then simply ask the prospect which one of them is the tangible bill, and which is the intangible.

Another effective approach when presenting your cost analysis is to *"net it out."* If your proposal represents an increase in expenses, your job is to justify to the prospect why it makes sense to pay more for your solution. You need to *"sell the difference."* Let's go a step further and make the increase in expenses digestible by netting it out. Let's say your $100,000 proposal is $12,000 per year *more* than the prospect is currently paying for existing methods. In order to make selling the difference easier, simply *minimize the increase* by breaking it down into smaller chunks. In this case, $12,000 a year is $1,000 per month, or only $45 per business day! Now all you have to do is justify $45 per day by high-lighting the benefits your solutions deliver. In the example above, if you can show just one hour of increased productivity per day, you've justified the investment.

If, on the other hand, your proposal shows a reduction of expenses, a savings, your job is to go the opposite direction and *maximize the savings* by multiplying the savings throughout the life of the product or agreement. For example, if you're saving your prospect $45 per day, that's $1,000 per month, $12,000 per year, and $60,000 over five years—the life span of the digital document management system.

It's a good day in sales when you can justify your proposal based on solid financial principles. In fact, in the example of the company in Amsterdam, when the salesperson finished writing the deal, the Chief Financial Officer asked him, "Is there any other place in my company you can do this for me?" It simply doesn't get any better than that!

At this point, you've future paced your prospect in your cover letter, validated the objectives and challenges, provided specifications on your solutions, and cost justified your proposal. Now it's time to turn the conversation toward closing the sale. The next two sections of your proposal will prompt you in this direction.

The next section of the winning proposal is a simple side-by-side "Benefits Summary" that compares and contrasts the prospect's current state with your proposed state. On the left side of the page under the heading of "Current State," simply list in bulleted points the downsides, inhibitors, and disadvantages of the prospect's current methods. On the right side simply list the upsides and benefits of your proposed solutions under the heading "Proposed State."

The last page in your proposal is the *final* Implementation Agenda that you and your prospect collaborated on during your last meeting when you presented your Executive Summary. At that time, you began to future pace your prospect by outlining the action steps required to implement your solutions. Now you've added steps, revised dates, and discussed the logistics of the transaction. Being at the final page in your proposal naturally puts you in the ideal position to again open the closing conversation.

Now that you've developed your winning proposal, it's time to design the accompanying value-proposition presentation that you will deliver along with your proposal.

PRESENT YOUR VALUE PROPOSITION: CRAFTING THE WINNING PRESENTATION

I see many salespeople supported by elaborate PowerPoint presentations; corporate capabilities brochures; and glossy marketing collateral with the company history, pictures of employees and the corporate headquarters, and client references. I'll present some ideas here that will help you transcend these conventional sales presentations, that your prospects have grown so accustomed to, and create competitive distinction during this stage of your sales process.

The good news is that if you devoted ample time and effort to crafting your positioning statement, you're well on you way to establishing the content for your value proposition presentation. In effect, your presentation is your positioning statement — on steroids! I suggest you use exactly this same format to compose your sales presentation.

Remember that the desired outcome of your presentation is to educate and inspire your prospect, create a sense of security, and address the prospect's concerns and issues so that they don't get brought up when it's time to close the sale. Let's revisit the elements of the positioning statement and then go on to add more elements that will help you craft a highly educational and compelling presentation.

Who Are You?

Again, from your work in the positioning statement, what are the three or four concise yet compelling words that define your company, beyond the name itself? In your presentation, define these words, expanding on your company's core competencies, market leadership, and overall business philosophy.

Also, be sure to define who you are individually. Describe your division and its mission. Define your personal role — expert resource, liaison, trusted advisor, go-to person — and define the outcomes you deliver to your customers.

What Business Are You In?

Remember, people don't buy products or services, they buy the outcome of the product or service. Present the final results you deliver your customers beyond the box, the service, or — as in the earlier example — the watch.

Remind prospects that they can buy the product or service anywhere, but that your company goes well beyond the product or service to deliver a total *customer experience*. Describe that customer experience. Go into detail about how your organization is uniquely qualified to deliver on that promise.

What's Unique?

Describe here what positions you way ahead of your competitors — what makes your product or service unique in the marketplace. You may present one or two aspects that your competition can't offer. It may be expertise, exclusive features your product or programs offer, or simply the way you do business.

One of the best sources for this information is your best customers. Interview them and ask them why they did business with you over your competition. Let them tell you from a customer's perspective what your unique competitive advantage is, and how they win as a result. (I'll address this in more detail in Chapter 12 on conducting account reviews.)

Whom Do You Do Business With, and What Results Do You Deliver?

Here's where you will transcend name-dropping and take full advantage of your references. Present industry-specific case studies that demonstrate your ability to consult, collaborate, and innovate, with the outcome of delivering stellar results for your customers.

Advertising research indicates that decision makers are interested in knowing about a vendor's expertise and ability to deliver measurable results in a similar industry. It's therefore critical that, when using references, you keep them specific to your prospect's industry or business environment.

Companies like IBM, Hewlett Packard, and Xerox are masters at this. You'll notice that their advertising campaigns will often have, at their core, case studies that describe a customer's business dilemma, what they did to solve it, and the results they delivered. Some of these ads run in publications that cost $100,000 for a full page in a single edition. Often you will see these companies take out four or five full-page ads with case studies anchoring the message, not marketing hype.

How Do You Deliver On Your Promise?

In your positioning statement, you briefly described your consultative sales process. Here, in the value proposition presentation, shift your emphasis to your organization's business model. Explain in detail how that model enables your organization to deliver on its promises.

Describe your company's infrastructure, internal processes, strategic partnerships, manufacturing facilities, service capabilities, and distribution systems that enable you to perform as stated. In effect, during this part of your presentation, you're touring the prospect through your organization. You're walking them through from start to finish, showing them every department, introducing them to internal resources, and putting the value-delivery-system puzzle together, step by step.

Your presentation should also include information on the value-added programs, guarantees, and customer-support services your organization offers. You may want to validate your company's leadership by providing management bios that present a team of qualified experts who are committed to providing the organization with long-term strategic vision, financial stability, and leadership.

PRODUCT DEMONSTRATIONS

Warning! If you only sell services, don't think this section doesn't apply to you! Sure, products have tangible buttons you can push to demonstrate a feature, which automatically prompts the salesperson to relate that feature to a benefit the prospect gains. However, it's important to recognize that insurance policies, consulting projects, and financial services all have tangible features and should be treated accordingly.

For example, the 24/7/365 roadside-assistance program is a feature of a customer-support program offered as added value with a Porsche Carrera. While it may be hard to demonstrate —and not as much fun—it is still as critical to building value in the presentation as the test drive that demonstrates the 320-horsepower engine.

Most product-demonstration training focuses on the traditional three-step approach of Feature–Application–Benefit (FAB). The button on a piece of equipment, the specification on a technology, or the feature of a service program prompts the salesperson to explain the Feature. The Application prompts the salesperson to explain *why the feature exists* in the first place. Under what applications or conditions would the user push the button or exercise the service feature? The Benefit is the desired result that the Feature delivers, the prize the user wins when they push the button or exercise the service feature.

I urge you, for every product demonstration or service-offering presentation you give, to make a list of the features you will be highlighting before you get face-to-face with your prospect. Next, ask yourself, "What does this button do? Why does the feature exist? What were the designers of the product or program thinking when they decided to incorporate the feature? Under what conditions would the prospect use this feature?" Then go on to list the benefits to the prospect when they use the feature or exercise the service offering.

For many of you, this is remedial. However, salespeople also need to be reminded of the basics that we all tend to let slide over the years. Product demonstrations and program presentations can become routine. While it may not be obvious to the salesperson, the prospect may be falling asleep or dying of boredom from the salesperson's lack of enthusiasm for the product or service being presented.

ONE MORE RANT ON CONTENT

Any prospect will tell you that there should be no such thing as a generic presentation or demonstration. Salespeople who simply drone on and on about every feature or every aspect of the program soon put prospects in a defensive mode. They are defending themselves against irrelevant information, someone wasting their precious time, and the risk of being bored to death!

All presentations or demonstrations should be tailored to your prospect's interests, based on what you know to be relevant from your discovery process. You need only emphasize those features and service offerings that help this individual prospect meet those unique objectives, remove challenges, and solve specific problems. If you spend precious time on features and programs that are not specific to your prospect, you'll not only dilute but also undermine the effectiveness of your presentation.

I understand that there are situations where including additional features and service offerings that are not central to the prospect's unique outcomes will add value to your proposal. But if you must present these features, hit them quickly, stress the likelihood of the application in the prospect's environment, and then tie the feature down to the benefit as "icing on the cake."

Now that you have a format for developing the content of your presentation and know what you want to say, let's take a look at some ideas on how to present that content in the most inspirational way possible.

THE DELIVERY
"It's not what you say, it's how you say it."

I begin my presentation seminars by asking the group to offer the characteristics of the most *memorable* presentations they've attended. I hear adjectives describing the best *presenters* as being enthusiastic, confident, in command of the material, interesting, humorous, animated, passionate, having flair, and to the point.

The *highest-impact* presentations are described as interactive, short and focused, tailored to the audience, and supported with creative stories and great visuals that facilitate retention of the material. Interestingly enough, few of these is related to *content!*

Conversely, when I solicit the characteristics of the *most annoying* presentations, I hear that the *presenter* read from notes, spoke in a monotone voice, was redundant, scattered, boring, went too long, presented too much irrelevant information, told old stories, or started with a lame joke. These presentations are described as lectures, held in a bad room, accompanied by bad visuals and handouts. Again, interestingly enough, most of these comments relate not to content, but to *delivery!*

So, what does this tell you about presentations? It's the same thing my mother used to tell me: "It's not what you say; it's how you say it."

I received my initial training in public speaking from Sue Gaulke, a corporate speaking coach who is the founder of Success Works and the Applause Speaker's Training Camp. Sue has written a book called *101 Ways to Captivate a Business Audience*. Sue's training and writing emphasize the importance of combining your presentation content with your delivery style. The goal of your presentation is to blend relevant content with inspiring delivery, so that the audience accepts and acts on your ideas.

Let's talk *style* first. Some of the most compelling arguments for the importance of style come from our personal experience in being on the receiving end of presentations. For most of us, whether or not we respond positively to a presentation depends largely on the presenter's *delivery style* and less on the *content!* Now I know that this may be a bit different in a one-on-one business setting or sales call, but still, you can't dismiss the stark reality implied here.

For many audiences, the speaker's effectiveness is dependent on *nonverbal* activities, such as appearance, gestures, eye contact, and enthusiasm. Another factor that influences effectiveness is the presenter's verbal skills, including articulation, word choice, and voice inflection. I've noticed that the presenter's effectiveness goes up dramatically if he or she stands up, instead of remaining seated.

It's also been proven that the audience's interest is highest during the presenter's introduction and conclusion and lowest in the body of the presentation. (Does this sound like you when you're in church or listening to the State of the Union Address?)

I'll share with you here some tips I've learned about giving high-impact presentations that combine content and delivery to put a turbo effect on your sales presentations.

THE INTRODUCTION

Unfortunately, many sales presentations start out something like this: "I'd like to begin by telling you about *our* company and *our* products and *our* services ... blah, blah, blah." It's no wonder at this point, just ten seconds into it that prospects look at their watch and think, "I wonder how long this is going to take."

The purpose of the introduction is to get the prospects' attention, reach out and grab them, bring them into the room, snap them out of their preoccupations and into your conversation. The best way I've found to do this (again via Sue Gaulke) is by using startling statistics that your discovery process revealed. For example:

- "During the next sixty minutes, as I present this proposal, your organization will spend $2,500 on telecommunications. That's right, $440,000 per month. That's $5,800,000 in the next year, if you do nothing about what I'm going to present in the next hour."

- "Today your company will have three claims filed in your employee benefits program. Each claim will take an average of eight hours to process. That's 6,040 hours per year consumed in the administration of claims. I'm here to help you reduce that by more than 30 percent."

149

▪ Or, as I heard a police chief appealing for increased budgets for fighting crime proclaim, "In the next thirty minutes, as we sit here in this room, there will be sixty-three crimes committed in our city—thirty-eight assaults, eighteen burglaries, five armed robberies and two rapes." Now do you think he has their attention?

Using relevant statistics that are specific to your audience will draw them in more quickly and deeply than any generic opening line or self-congratulatory proclamation about your company or even a gratuitous compliment paid to your audience.

THE BODY

Now that you have your prospect's attention, it's your job to hold that interest. This can be some heavy lifting for both you and the prospect. I know that after many deliveries, you have your presentation down pat and delivery is like an out-of body-experience. It just seems to flow without much effort. Your command of the information is obvious, and your effectiveness is secure.

Still, I encourage you to beware of the coma-like trance that even the best rock-and-roll acts are susceptible to; many times they appear to *"phone it in."* Stand up. Be animated and passionate. Use your voice and your visuals to show your conviction in the value you, your organization, and your products, services, and programs deliver to your clients.

Whether you're presenting information from slides or from a bound document, it's critical to preface the information on each slide or page with *why* the information is important to the audience. Once you present the information, close each slide or page with, *"What this means to you is* _____ *,"* filling in the blank with a compelling benefit tie-down statement.

THE CONCLUSION

After presenting a compelling business case for why your prospect should hire you and your organization to implement the solutions you are proposing, it's time to inspire the prospect to act on your ideas and proposal. Like any good preacher, you should have an inspirational benediction that moves your audience beyond, "That's good information," to "What do you want me to do next?"

Begin your closing statements by briefly restating the statistics from your introduction. Summarize the prospect's objectives, challenges, and problem areas. Summarize your solutions, emphasizing the benefits to the prospect of acting on your proposal. Next, stage the finale. Explain the logistics of implementing your proposal. Lace the conversation with projections that position you as the assumed resource. You may say, "Once we implement these solutions, I will monitor the results. Then you and I will collaborate further to determine the next few priorities going forward."

I suggest that in closing your presentation you review your entire consulting and collaborative process and acknowledge your prospect for the time and effort they've contributed to that process. Next, thank your prospect for the opportunity to travel the road together, and then simply ask if they have all the necessary information they need in order to take the next step.

SOME FINAL THOUGHTS ON DELIVERY

Like so many aspects of successful selling behavior, sales presentations are as much about the nuances of delivery as they are about the content within. Here are some ideas on delivering presentations that will increase your impact.

The Venue

The most successful sales eagles I know always take the extra effort to assure they have the home-field advantage by arranging their presentations at their own facilities. Now we all know the challenges and potential expenses associated with getting decision makers to travel to your office or locations such as hotel conference rooms or private clubs. I can assure you however that doing this justifies the effort.

First of all, in your own venue, you have total control of the environment, interruptions, audio-visual equipment, demonstration technology, and, most importantly, the timing of the presentation.

Many sales organizations design organizational tours and set up conference facilities with their sales presentations in mind. They have catering services for morning and lunchtime presentations. This helps create the perfect environment for building rapport and putting everyone at ease prior to the presentation.

As I mentioned earlier, conducting organizational tours as part of your presentation helps you present your business model, delivery system, infrastructure, management team, products, and your proposal in the best possible showcase.

Once my clients adopt this home-field advantage and steadfastly adhere to it, they enjoy closing ratios of over 80 percent, compared to 40 to 50 percent closing rates when presentations are given in the prospect's office.

Memorize Your Introduction and Conclusion

I've delivered hundreds of public speeches to groups ranging in size from twenty-five to 3,000. Even after hundreds of appearances, just moments before the start my nerves begin to chatter. During the first one to two minutes of the presentation, they are shouting. Once I get beyond the introduction and into the body of the presentation, I have that out-of-body experience and simply go with it. Then, toward the end as I approach the conclusion, my nerves start to taunt me, because I know I've got to nail the landing.

One tip I've adopted and practice religiously is to memorize my introduction and conclusion verbatim, rehearse them relentlessly, and *never deviate* from them, regardless of the circumstances. Remember, the audience's interest is highest in these two parts of your show, so don't let them down. Demonstrate your confidence and conviction in the opening act, deliver your content in the second act, and finish the show with a composed, confident, and compelling closing scene.

IT'S SHOW TIME!
WHICH COMES FIRST, THE CHICKEN OR THE EGG?

Here you are in the process. It is well after discovery, after your initial consulting engagement where you presented your discovery findings and your recommendations for improving the prospect's business with your solutions. You've collaborated with your prospect and prioritized which of your recommendations to propose. You've positioned yourself as the consultant and now have a tremendous amount of momentum going into the next meeting to present your proposal.

It's at this point that you have to make a critical decision. Are you going to behave in the traditional way salespeople are trained to behave, or are you going to "misbehave" and try something new?

Give Them the Price First!

I know what you're thinking, "What? Are you crazy?" But hear me out before you decide. Bill Pope sells commercial insurance in San Diego, California. He's one of the best salespeople I've ever met. Bill nearly started a street riot at one of my conferences where we had sales eagles sharing best practices.

Bill stood up and proclaimed that his best practice was to give the decision maker the price page from his proposal *before* he gave his value-proposition presentation. Bill insisted that prospects don't pay attention to your presentation until they have some frame of reference as to the financial feasibility of your proposal. He backed up this point by asking the group, "When you hand a prospect a bound proposal with ten to fifteen pages of presentation content in the front, what's the first thing they do?" Unanimously, the group roared back, "Flip through the document to the price page!" Bill responded, "Exactly. Why fight human nature?"

Even with the group's resounding agreement with this argument, 50 percent insisted that the best way to present proposals was to build the value first and then present the price. The other 50 percent of the eagles insisted, along with Bill, that the prospect is not engaged in your value-proposition presentation until they know the price, so why not give it to them first?

Show your prospects in black and white what they are currently paying to have objectives unmet and challenges unresolved. Then, show them what they would be paying for your solutions. You either represent an increase or a decrease in operating costs. Either way, you simply show them the facts and then ask them, "Based on these numbers, are you interested in the presentation of my value proposition related to this proposal?"

In the *PowerSelling* model, I say harness your momentum and remain in the consultative role throughout the entire process, again keeping the focus on your prospect's needs and desires instead of your own. This means choosing the contrarian's path and presenting your proposal prior to presenting your company's capabilities and your value propositions.

Sample
Winning Proposal Format
Cover Letter

Prospect's name   Date
Title
Organization

Thank you for the opportunity to consult and collaborate on the issues of [your industry] for [prospect's organization]. I appreciate your participation and contribution in the process that has led to my submission of the attached proposal.

In our last meeting, we reviewed the Executive Summary and prioritized those problem areas that you deemed critical to address. We also reviewed the related Implementation Agenda for phasing in the proposed solutions. The first action item on the agenda was to review and approve the proposal, putting the implementation process into motion.

The attached proposal includes:

- Objectives and Challenges

- Descriptions of solutions, products, and scope of services

- Operating-costs analysis

- Investment justification

- Benefits summary

- Final Implementation Agenda

- Sample contracts and documentation

- Value-proposition support collateral

I look forward to presenting our solutions, reviewing the financial offer, and discussing the logistics of implementation. Again, I encourage your input as to how we can work together toward a favorable decision and a long-term working relationship.

Seller's name
Title
Organization

Sample
Winning Proposal Format
Overview of Objectives and Challenges

Briefly list *edited* objectives and challenges from the Executive Summary in a bulleted format.

Objectives

-
-
-
-

Challenges

-
-
-
-

Sample
Winning Proposal Format
Solutions, Specifications, and Support

Provide an in-depth description of:

■ Product/technology specifications

■ Scope of services

■ Client support programs

■ Warranties

■ Guarantees

■ Installation and training

■ Ongoing support

■ Financial Offer

  – Acquisition options

  – Financing terms

  – Fee based a la carte options

  – Added value bundled into the proposal

Sample
Winning Proposal Format
Operating Costs Analysis

Current Operating Costs	Proposed Operating Cost
Itemize all elements of operating costs related to current methods in monthly or annual figures	Itemize all elements of operating costs related to proposed methods in monthly or annual figures

Current Operating Costs		**Proposed Operating Costs**	
_____	$ _____	_____	$ _____
_____	$ _____	_____	$ _____
_____	$ _____	_____	$ _____
_____	$ _____	_____	$ _____
_____	$ _____	_____	$ _____
_____	$ _____	_____	$ _____

Total Current Operating Costs $ _____   **Total Proposed Operating Costs** $ _____

Monthly Increase/Decrease $ _____
Annual Increase/Decrease $ _____

Sample
Winning Proposal Format
Investment Justification

Demonstrate in black and white how your proposal is cost justified via the payback/breakeven, ROI, or Cash-Flow Analysis.

Payback/breakeven Model

Payback/ Breakeven Formula: $$\frac{\text{monthly or annual savings}}{\text{initial investment}} = \text{payback}$$

Return on Investment Model

Return on Investment Formula: $$\frac{\text{average annual net pre-tax income or costs savings}}{\substack{\text{cost of proposed investment} \\ \text{(project costs)}}} = \text{ROI percentage}$$

Cash-Flow Analysis

Example: Existing telecom system with $1 million replacement cost in year three and annual operating costs of $125,000 per year.

Year 1	Year 2	Year 3	Year 4	Year 5	Total over 5 years
$125,000	$125,000	$1,125,000	$125,000	$125,000	= $1,625,000

New telecom system with $1 million replacement costs in year one and annual operating costs of $25,000 per year. (This is a $100,000 per year savings in operating cost for five years.)

Year 1	Year 2	Year 3	Year 4	Year 5	Total over 5 years
$1,025,000	$25,000	$25,000	$25,000	$25,000	= $1,125,000

Net savings = $500,000 over 5 years starting in year one.

Sample
Winning Proposal Format
Benefits Summary

Current State	Proposed State
List downsides, inhibitors, disadvantages of current state	**List benefits related to proposed solutions**

Current State	Proposed State
▨ Objectives not met	▨ Objectives met
▨ Challenges unresolved	▨ Challenges resolved
▨ Excessive operating costs	▨ Reduced operating costs leading to increased profits
▨ Waste	▨ Elimination of waste
▨ Redundancy	▨ Elimination of redundancy
▨ User contention	▨ Improved quality
▨ Sub standard quality	▨ Reduced expenses and time related to vendor administration
▨ Expenses and time related to vendor administration	

Sample
Winning Proposal Format
Final Implementation Agenda

List all revised action items and revised dates from your last collaboration and review of the Implementation Agenda in your Executive Summary.

Action Items   **Proposed Completion Dates**

Sample
Winning Proposal Format
Sample Contracts and Documentation

Provide actual or sample contracts and documentation required by your organization in order to finalize the transaction.

Sample
Winning Proposal Format
Value Proposition Support Collateral

Provide marketing collateral, supporting evidence, case studies, corporate capabilities and product brochures, management bios, and detailed information related to your value proposition.

CHAPTER 10

Collaborate to
Resolve Obstacles

How challenging would the game of golf be without sand traps? When the game becomes more challenging, it also becomes more interesting. To make it even more challenging, and interesting, sand traps are usually placed right in front of your ultimate goal, the green.

In sales, your ultimate goal is the close. And, just as in golf, the closer you get to the goal, the more challenging and interesting the endeavor becomes. This is where you often land in the sand trap, where your prospect surrounds the goal with issues, concerns, or even flat-out objections to your ideas.

In golf there are special tools, like the sand wedge, and skills required to get up and out of the trap successfully. In sales, when working with prospects to resolve issues, handle objections, and negotiate final details of the sale, there are also tools and skills required to achieve the desired win/win result. I guarantee that once you become familiar with the tools presented here and practice these techniques, your already challenging sales career will become much more interesting.

THREE CORNERSTONES FOR SUCCESS: ANTICIPATE, RESPOND VERSUS REACT, AND COLLABORATE

The first cornerstone for successfully navigating issues or obstacles during the close is to know and anticipate which ones you will face most often. You want to eliminate the element of surprise and the normal reaction of retreat. The second cornerstone is to develop effective responses to the most common issues, concerns, and objections you will face. You want to be thoroughly prepared to respond quickly and intelligently. Third, you must be prepared to continue working together in the *collaborative mode,* even when your prospect enters into a *negotiation mode.*

Years ago when I was a sales manager for a document technology organization, I was assigned to launch a new product in the marketplace. I was managing a sales force of mostly new salespeople. It soon became obvious that every time a salesperson faced an objection, he or she would retreat back to the safety of the office. Objections were literally scaring them away from potential sales.

After about ninety days of total failure, I implemented a daily routine that quickly resulted in a dramatic turnaround and one of the most successful product launches in the history of the company. Since then, I've encouraged all my clients to use this simple exercise to help their salespeople anticipate, respond, and collaborate with prospects to overcome obstacles and move forward to close any sale.

First, to identify the most common obstacles, I began a month-long project of listing each obstacle onto a master log posted in the sales office. Each day the salespeople would return from the field and post the issues, concerns, and objections they encountered: "I'm not interested," "I need to shop around," "Your price is too high," "I have to think about it," "I'll call you when I make a decision," and "We've decided not to decide at this time" were just a few postings.

Then, once a week at our sales meeting, we would review the list, and I would lead a brainstorming session to develop effective responses for each obstacle. After a few weeks, the place looked like a war room. Flip-chart pages wallpapered the office with objections and responses. Every day salespeople role-played new responses before picking up the phone or going into the field. We changed our prospecting approach and sales presentation, incorporating evidence and information that short-circuited known obstacles in advance.

Through the course of this exercise, it became obvious that most of the obstacles fell into one of the three categories described in the prospecting section of this book: Prospects didn't see a need for the product or didn't see a *need* to change their current methods, they didn't see a *value* in our proposal, or they were *fearful* of making a decision or changing their current situation.

THE PROSPECT DOESN'T NEED TO MAKE A DECISION NOW

First, let's take a look at need-based obstacles that result in a lack of urgency on the prospect's part after you've presented your proposal. Obviously, since you've fully engaged prospects up to this point, they see the need for your product or service. What they don't see is the need to make a decision now. At this point, it's up to you to create urgency to accelerate a favorable decision.

To create a sense of urgency, you need to revisit certain parts of your presentation and proposal to reinforce key points. You need to point out to your prospect that *not* going ahead with your proposal will cause them to miss immediate opportunities to increase productivity, reduce costs, improve quality, or realize a return on investment.

For example, if prospects are spending money on a current system or methods that don't offer the benefits your proposal provides, you're only asking them to invest in the difference between what they are currently spending and what your proposal requires. Remind your prospects that these current methods are hindering them from meeting their stated objectives, and that doing nothing only invites the inevitable impacts of not addressing problem areas.

It's obvious that this kind of response will only work if you've been thorough and competent in your consultative discovery process and if your proposal incorporates the prospect's own evidence of the organization's objectives, challenges, impacts, and problem areas.

Again, use evidence to support your arguments. Refer to your Executive Summary, ROI, payback or cash-flow analysis. Revisit the portions of your presentation that summarize the benefits to the prospect of making a decision now.

After all this education and reinforcement, your prospects may be feeling better about how the facts support your arguments. They may even be leaning toward your position, but still not ready to commit. Here's where some inspiration on your part may be required. Many times the prospect simply needs a nudge or a good reason to move your proposal along in the priority parade of decisions at hand. It's at this point that many traditional salespeople will resort to offering a discount in exchange for a timely decision.

In the *PowerSelling* model, I encourage you to add *value-base incentives* to your proposal to create the urgency necessary to close the sale now. Perhaps you can add value with some flexibility in your financial terms, warranty extensions, bundling of accessories or related products or services, packaging additional quantities, or offering additional support programs.

When offering incentives to create urgency, you must build a credible business case for how you are able to provide the incentive. You must also attach a deadline to the offer.

For example, if your company has received favorable payment terms from your supplier, you may be in a position to pass those terms on to your customers who take delivery by the deadline date. Or perhaps you're able to bundle some related accessories or products into your proposal due to an inventory level that must be reduced by the end of the quarter. If you're selling services, you may be in a position to add-value by protecting the prospect from price increases that are pending in your industry.

In short, when dealing with need-based obstacles, you need to educate your prospect to validate that the need exists, reinforce your cost justification, and be prepared to *create urgency* to inspire your prospect to act now.

THE PROSPECT DOESN'T SEE A VALUE

Next, let's examine value-based obstacles. They can sound something like, "This is more money than I had in mind," "Your price is too high," or even worse, "Your price is higher than your competitor's." However articulated, what the prospect is really saying is, "I don't see the full value in your proposal," or, "I don't see that the benefits of your product or service offset the costs."

Again, many salespeople go straight to discounting their price as the only way to handle this objection. In fact, many salespeople think that they have to get their price down to what the prospect wants to pay or, in a competitive situation, meet or beat the competitor's price in order to close the sale.

Here again is where you need to have an effective response ready and be skilled in walking through a collaborative process with your prospect. In dealing with value-based obstacles, education is again critical. You'll need to revisit the prospect's current operating cost and sell only the difference by referring to your cost-justification models. Remember to reduce any increase in costs to a digestible number by presenting it as a daily, hourly, or per-usage cost.

For example, if your price for a fractional jet lease is $5,000 per trip more than the prospect is paying for commercial flights for their top executives, you can reduce this to an hourly number to cost-justify the difference. If the average travel time is six hours, and normally four executives travel together, that constitutes twenty-four hours of executive time or productivity. Let's say your jet service reduces travel time by 25 percent. That saves your prospect six hours of executive productivity. Now your proposal is only $208 per hour more than commercial travel. Surely your prospects value the executives' time at a substantially higher amount.

Now let's look at the situation when your competitor's price comes into play. When your proposal is higher than your competitor's, it's your challenge and your job to sell the additional value that your product, services, and organization deliver. First, before you even think of meeting or beating your competitor's price, make absolutely sure that your prospect is comparing apples to apples, pound for pound, and program for program.

I've seen hundreds of cases where, upon full disclosure and additional discovery, it's no mystery why the competitor's price is lower. Maybe the competition offers fewer features, shorter warranties, lower quality, or fee-based a la carte support programs. Perhaps its proposals hide financing costs or delivery and training fees. I've seen competitors package product with sub-conventional yields or quantities. For example, when the industry's standard packaging is twenty-four units per case, they may package twenty units per case. Always, always, always know exactly what you're up against, even if it means calling your prospect's hand and requesting to see the competitor's proposals, specifications, and terms before you respond.

Next, let's say that your prospect is comparing apples to

apples and that your price is in fact higher than your competitor's. Instead of just discounting your price to meet or beat that price, you must ask your prospect this critical question: "If my price was exactly the same as the competition's price, and you had to make a decision today, to whom would you award the business?"

If the prospect says, "Well, if that's the case, I'd give you the business," they must see some additional value in your product, service, organization, or proposal. Your response should then be, "You obviously see some additional value in my proposal. What do you see that warrants giving me the business?" Once you've identified the competitive distinction, it's your job to attach a monetary value to that distinction, thus justifying the higher price. Now, you still might not get 100 percent of your *value-distinction premium*, but at this point you certainly don't need to meet or beat the competitor's price to win the business.

Again, be prepared to offer a nudge, create some urgency, and close the business before the prospect cools off or the competition gets back in and takes an even more aggressive position. If there's enough flexibility in your pricing to compromise and meet the prospect in the middle, or to offer more attractive terms, or bundle some added value, now is the time and the place to do it.

THE PROSPECT IS FEARFUL OF MAKING A DECISION

Finally, if your prospects offer fear-based objections, it usually means that they are afraid of change, making the wrong decision, or facing the unknown. Prospects who are paralyzed by fear may say things like, "We have some concerns about going ahead," or, "I'm hesitant to change vendors or methods or enter into a long-term agreement," or, even worse, "We've decided not to decide at this time."

Once again, education is the first avenue of response. You must offer plenty of supporting evidence and layers of security blankets. Revisit your ROI or payback model. Be ready to provide names of references that have made similar decisions and lived to tell the story. Provide references who will testify on your behalf as to your credibility and to the results you've delivered.

Offer further security through written guarantees that your organization will deliver the proposed results. You may have to offer a money-back policy in the event that you don't. Guarantees reverse the risk from the customer to the vendor and therefore remove the element of fear. Since they were first introduced by Sears, Roebuck and Company in the late 1800s, guarantees have been one of the most effective marketing tools ever created.

I know money-back guarantees and escape clauses are not possible in some businesses, such as commercial real estate, rocket launches, and sales training, but don't let your legal department throw a wet blanket on this powerful risk-reversal tool.

EIGHT TIPS ON HANDLING CONCERNS & OBJECTIONS

1. **Relax.** When a prospect voices concerns or objections, don't react. Relax, sit back in your chair, and even smile for a few seconds as you prepare to *respond*.

2. **Validate.** Don't get defensive or launch into an immediate response. First, validate your prospect's concern by saying, "That's an interesting point. I'm glad you brought it up. It shows that you're interested."

3. **Explore.** Suggest that both you and the prospect work together to discover the reason the concern exists. Say something like, "Let's explore that and determine exactly why my price may seem higher than my competitor's."

4. **Isolate.** Isolate this concern as the only issue between you and the yes decision by asking, "Is this the only concern you have before you make a decision?"

5. **Review the presentation.** Always get back to education, revisiting only those elements of your presentation, proposal, guarantees, etc., that offer the supporting evidence for your response. Try saying, "Let's review the facts related to this issue."

6. **Prove the value.** Summarize the benefits of your proposal, highlighting those elements that address the concern and validate the added-value your solution and proposal offer.

7. **Close.** Revisit the decision-making process and remind your prospect that this is not a spontaneous decision. You could say, "You've seen the unique benefits we provide and you've agreed that we offer more value and support. I've included some financial incentives and I've addressed your concerns. Are you comfortable making a decision at this point?"

8. **Be prepared to negotiate.** Even after effectively handling the objection, be prepared for the buyer who is looking for one more nudge, or even worse, the buyer who is trained to get the best deal for their organization. Always, always, always have one more card to play, one more incentive, even if it's a minor one.

NEGOTIATION:
BE PREPARED TO NEGOTIATE!

To negotiate means to confer with another in order to come to terms, to arrange or settle by agreement. In more than twenty-five years in sales, I've learned that the deeper your rapport with your prospect, and the more consultative and collaborative your sales process, the more your prospect will view you as an advocate.

I've also found that when you combine deep rapport and a consultative process with sound articulation of your business case, supported with cost justifications and implementation schedules, the less need there is for negotiation skills. It simply doesn't come up as often as it does when the buyer doesn't feel part of the process, presentations are generic, proposals are product-price quotations, and valid objections are dismissed with nonsensical responses.

That being said, I've also learned to expect some negotiation at the end of every customer engagement. I view negotiation as a favorable part of the process. This is closing. It's simply a step in collaborating and coming to terms, or settling by agreement. To effectively negotiate an agreement, one must enter the negotiation with a truly collaborative attitude.

One of the first things you must understand is that for many decision makers, especially trained professionals in finance or purchasing, negotiation is a requirement of the job. Their organizations have stated policies mandating that no agreement will be entered into without making the best effort to secure the best price, terms, and value possible. Many organizations provide their decision makers with professional training in negotiation skills and processes to this end. It's simply good business.

A DETOUR

On a recent visit to Hong Kong I received some negotiation training from an antique collector who offered his advice while I was looking to buy some antique Chinese chairs for my home. He explained that in Asia, negotiation is an art form and that cultural rules must be strictly adhered to. The lessons I learned apply anywhere. First, know the rules of the game. Second, know your final objective or outcome—the desired price or offer—before you engage. And third, always allow the other party to "save face."

What are the rules of the game? First, there must be a willingness to accept, allow, and even facilitate a win/win outcome for both parties. It's not about beating someone by being better than they are. It's about reaching a fair agreement so that both parties walk away with their objectives met. Knowing the rules of the game also means understanding the negotiation process.

My Hong Kong advisor educated me on how shop owners price their furniture at the highest-possible asking price, knowing that the process of negotiation will adjust the final price far below that. Therefore, it was my job to make my initial offer at around 25 percent of the asking price and trust that the process would adjust the final price close to the 50 percent mark. It was made clear to me, however, that getting to that middle ground could take considerable time and effort.

I was also coached on deciding what my final offer for the chairs was going to be before I engaged in the process and on being absolutely willing to walk from the deal if I didn't arrive at that price. This way, I wouldn't let an emotional attachment to the chairs get in the way of good business sense.

Saving face is a cultural principle in Asia. You must always allow the other party a formal and graceful rejection of your offer, never an outright objection or rejection. I was instructed to make the first move. My offer was to be written down on a piece of paper, folded up, and hand-delivered to the shop owner. The shop owner then smiled and instructed my wife and I to return to the shop in thirty to forty minutes, after he had reviewed and considered my offer.

When we returned, the shop owner graciously offered us tea and calmly stated his business case and the details as to how he had arrived at his asking price for the chairs. He then acknowledged our offer as appreciated, but unacceptable, and asked if he could formally present his counteroffer. He took the same piece of paper and crossed out our number, wrote his new offer, folded the paper back up and formally presented it back to us. We smiled, took the paper, and said we would need some time to consider the offer and would return in thirty to forty minutes with our decision.

This was work. Following the rules of the game, understanding the negotiation process, and allowing each other to save face took time and effort. After four hours of going back and forth; five cups of tea; and endless education on the history of China, the DNA of the chairs, the logistics of their refurbishment, and the cost associated with the crating, shipping, and insurance we struck a deal smack in the middle of where we both started. We were both happy. We had both achieved our objectives, done our jobs for our respective organizations, and no one lost face in the process.

BACK TO THE TOPIC

The point is that both you and your prospect have a job to do. You'll have to go through a process and work together to meet in the middle. In my experience, the following negotiation techniques help accelerate the process and assure a successful outcome for both parties:

Let the Other Party Go First

At a minimum, by letting the other party go first, you know how far apart you are before you make your concession or counteroffer. I've been shocked many times at the responses I've heard once prospects volunteer their positions. Countless times I've encountered prospects who were agreeable with the price but simply wanted more favorable terms or slightly more value added to the deal.

Acknowledge the Other Party's Point

This is a simple technique taught in every high school debate class. Instead of lunging into your own response, recognize the other person's position, by simply saying, "I see your point and understand that your job is to secure the best possible deal for your organization."

Confirm and Isolate the Prospect's Point

To make sure that there are no new cards to be played, simply ask, "If we can settle on this issue of _____, are you prepared to take the final step?"

Articulate Your Value Proposition

Here you must build your business case for how you determined your price. You must restate the value and the benefits the prospect achieves in exchange for this price. In other words, acknowledge your value and tell the prospect why you're worth it. Like the shop owner, you must engage and educate prospects and get them to acknowledge the *overall value* of your proposal.

Graciously Decline Unacceptable Offers

You can say, "Based on what I just presented, I appreciate, but can't accept, your proposal. I would, however, like to present a counteroffer, because I think we're getting close."

Present Your Counteroffer

If you've left yourself some room and you're close to a win/win settlement, it's time to close the deal. Remember, your prospect has a job to do and this is simply part of the process. At this point, present your counteroffer, acknowledging what adjustments in price, terms, or added value you are willing to exchange for a favorable decision *now*. Let's say that you're not far from a fair deal and you've left yourself some wiggle room, knowing that some negotiation was inevitable or at least probable. In many cases it comes down to both parties meeting in the middle. In an effort to have your prospect come halfway, try this, "I realize you have a job to do for your organization, and that is to get the best possible overall value. I have that same job at my organization, and that's to arrive at the best possible transaction. Most people I work with in your position are fair-minded. When I offer to meet them in the middle, they see that offer as fair. Will you come halfway so that we can shake hands in the middle?"

Know When to Walk

I guarantee that eight out of ten times meeting in the middle will work for both you and your prospect. But it's not a perfect world, so two times out of ten you'll run into buyers who believe that you must lose in order for them to win. They not only won't meet you in the middle, they will grind you for the best price, dictate the terms, plus tell you how to run your business. There are times you need to know when to call a time out, and times you need to know when to walk out.

Before I walk out, I like to call a time out or stage a "take-away" close. A take-away is when you pull the proposal off the table, step back, and release the pressure. A simple take-away goes something like this: "Maybe this isn't the right time for you," or "Maybe you're not ready for this," or "Maybe you can't afford this right now. It's best at this point, that I table this offer until the timing is better."

Watch what happens with take-away closes. Many times, prospects now want what they can't have and come at you with a more appropriate counteroffer. Now you both win. On the other hand, they may go the other direction and ask you to walk. Either way, I love take-aways, because at least you get a definitive answer.

In conclusion, I repeat my opening mantra: If you develop a deep rapport with your prospects, position yourself as their consultative resource, offer them valuable information during your process, articulate your value proposition well, and cost justify your proposed solutions, you'll find yourself negotiating only small implementation logistics, and not big deal-killing issues, this late in the process.

Collaborate for the "Anti-Climactic" Close

By future pacing the prospect with your Implementation Agenda, closing should be anti-climactic, a natural extension of previous conversations, collaborations, negotiations, and agreements.

You've collaborated with the prospect to identify the steps both organizations must take in order to implement the solutions. You've documented those steps and attached dates in your Implementation Agenda. You've engaged your prospect to prioritize your recommendations and provided a sound cost justification.

If the prospect has had concerns, push-backs, or even outright objections, they would have come up loud and clear by now. You would have collaborated and negotiated through them effectively, skillfully isolating them to avoid any last-minute surprises.

During the discussions of the Implementation Agenda, you've introduced the concept of finalizing the transaction via "documentation." Many salespeople I train include copies of their contracts, credit applications, lease agreements, etc. in their proposals and encourage the prospect to review them prior to the documentation date.

THE THREE-STEP CLOSE

Even with all the consulting, collaboration, future pacing, and engagement, closing is often a nerve-racking event for both buyers and sellers. Buyers know that it's decision time and that they must now walk over the threshold. Sellers know that they have done everything possible to make that decision low-risk and high-reward. At the same time, both parties experience a business adrenaline rush just prior to asking for and making this commitment.

I steadfastly recommend that you master the following three-step closing process to assure that you are prepared to close when the time comes. First, you must open the closing conversation. Second, you must deliver your closing line. Third, you must ask for and take action.

Opening the Closing Conversation

As presented earlier, the Implementation Agenda is the initial opening of the closing conversation. In this stage of the process, you need to choreograph the finalization of the process carefully. First, you must address the tension that naturally builds in the prospect's mind just prior to making a commitment.

The most effective way to calm a buyer is to briefly review the entire process that has brought you both to this decision threshold. This reassures prospects that they are not jumping into the commitment without due diligence. Your job is to remind them that they have engaged in a thorough process en route to making a sound business decision. This is simple. I'll even provide some verbiage that will prompt and support you in implementation.

In reviewing the steps that you both took to arrive at this point, simply start at the beginning and summarize each stage of your consultative sales process. Simply say, "Before we get to the final details, I want to briefly review how we got here. First, after getting to know each other, I gained a clear understanding of your organization during my comprehensive discovery process. I then documented my discovery findings in the Executive Summary. We then collaborated on the recommendations, prioritizing which recommendations you wanted to implement first. Then, I proposed and cost-justified those solutions, and we discussed implementation and our ongoing account reviews. During this entire process, you've been extremely thorough and helpful."

Deliver the Closing Line

I have been out on countless sales calls with salespeople who, at the final moment of truth, end up babbling out some vague or even incoherent statement about closing the sale. Or even worse, they don't say anything. The prospect feels the tension escalate to a seemingly unbearable level, comes up with an escape plan, and says something like, "I'll have to think about it and get back to you."

No matter how good you are, how much experience you have, and how much confidence you have in your proposal, it helps to have some patented closing lines that will help you stay focused and inspire your prospect to take that final step over the threshold to commitment. Here's a sampling of closing lines that I know are highly effective and consistent with the *PowerSelling* model of consulting and collaborating to gain competitive distinction:

- "Here we are at the first step in the implementation. Now that you've seen all the facts, all the numbers, the cost justification, and the benefits of this proposal, is this something you're ready to move forward on now?"

- "Based on this proposal and cost justification, do we

have a basis for moving forward to the next step, which is to convert this proposal to documentation and finalize the details?"

- "Based on our Implementation Agenda, the next step in the process is for you to approve this proposal. Is this proposal acceptable to you? If so, all we have to do is shake hands and take care of the documentation."

- "Based on everything we've discussed, I have two questions for you: Do you have all the information necessary to make a decision, and do you feel comfortable at this point making a decision?"

- "There are just a couple of details left in order to implement these solutions. First, we shake hands, then execute the documents. Are we at that point?"

And now, a light close from one of the best salespeople I've ever worked with.

- "I feel like we've been on a journey together. Are we there yet?"

I encourage you to shamelessly steal a couple of these closing lines or craft two that fit your personality. Practice them diligently until you can recite them falling off a barstool. Only then will you have the confidence and skill to deliver them smoothly and seamlessly in front of a prospect at the moment of truth.

Ask for and Take Action

In my sales management career, I personally rode out on more than 5,700 sales calls where I was face-to-face with the decision maker. Usually I was there to support my salesperson in closing the business. I personally closed or witnessed more than 1,900 closed sales and I can remember only two times when prospects actually closed themselves. One guy asked us, "Do you need a check now?" The other surprised us by asking, "Do you have something for me to sign?" After we picked ourselves up off the floor we said, "Well, er, yes."

Even after a stellar execution of the process and all the rehearsed opening and closing lines, don't expect your prospect to offer to make the first move toward documentation. Here's where many salespeople actually create their own disconnect, through simple lack of action. If you've set this up properly, your prospect has seen the documentation and reviewed the terms and conditions in advance. Based on your Implementation Agenda, the prospect is expecting *you* to formally close the transaction *now*.

Every organization — both the buyer's and seller's — has different documentation and related processes for formally closing a transaction. If your sale is document-intensive, and both yours and the prospect's organizations must dance their way through contracts, lease agreements, credit applications, etc., I suggest that you first get a letter of commitment signed that confirms this documentation process and target dates for completion. Include this as an addendum to the Implementation Agenda.

If your organization can enter into an agreement with a simple contract and signature, then take the contract out and lay it on the desk now. Or, even better, take it out and lay it on the desk before you open the closing conversation and review your consultative sales process. This will send the signal early that you are there to do business.

I've listened to salespeople explain why they practically melt down at closing time. They postpone the closing conversation, hoping that the prospect will volunteer to buy or at least give a verbal approval, signaling the go-ahead to bring the contracts out of the briefcase.

When I ask them, "What are you afraid of? What's the worst that could happen?" they tell me that by applying any pressure at all at this point, they could risk blowing the sale. I respond to this by saying that without at least trying to close, there is no sale to blow!

The key word here is pressure. One must not look at asking for action as pressure, and I don't think that asking for action at this point is in any way pressure. Pressure is a tactic that incompetent salespeople resort to as part of their unilateral and manipulative sales process. Any sales professional will agree that after engaging in a consultative and collaborative sales process, it is at this point that you've "earned the right" to a decision, and a favorable one at that.

Even in my Hong Kong experience, after many hours of collaboration, abiding by the rules of engagement, and allowing each party to save face at the end of the process, I was ready to buy the chairs. But I wasn't going to offer to take the next step. It was only after the shop owner and I agreed on a final offer and discussed the final shipping logistics that he casually asked me which credit card I would use to pay. It was the way he so kindly asked me for the card that closed the deal.

For many who have been through my *PowerSelling* training, it's no surprise that closing is the shortest chapter in the book. That's not because closing is unimportant, or that a consultative and collaborative sales process and field tools such as Implementation Agendas make closing easy, an automatic, uncontested result. Closing is like putting in golf. There are golf pros with incredible distance-driving capacity, iron shots to die for, and chipping skills that consistently assure short, easy putts. Yet I've seen plenty of these pros blow a championship by missing a three-foot putt. They were so sure about the final step that they ended up forsaking the fundamentals and assuming the desired result.

Closing is a skill. The three steps and actual closing verbiages offered here are fundamental to the *PowerSelling* process. Your total command of the process, tools, and delivery of the verbiage will require practice, trial, and adjustment to your personality and circumstances. It is only then that you can implement the process successfully, use the tools skillfully, and develop the confidence to stage and deliver your close effectively.

Expand Your Opportunity via Account Reviews: The Sale Has Just Begun

U nfortunately for many salespeople, closing the sale means a brief celebration, and then jumping on the treadmill and running to the next prospective account to start the process all over again. This is understandable, since their compensation program encourages them to become heat-seeking missiles, always identifying and striking the next hot target. Or their sales manager quickly reminds them that it's a thirty-day war out there, and the new month has just begun.

At this point, many salespeople will actively engage in prospecting or rely on their marketing resources to generate new selling opportunities. As I have traveled the world working with veteran eagles, I have discovered one behavior they have in common that constantly keeps them in selling opportunities. They are religious about conducting account reviews.

Eagles realize there are two reasons for conducting comprehensive account reviews with clients on an ongoing basis. First, they open doors to new opportunities to expand your reach within the account. Second, it paves the way to earn the right to gain high-quality referrals.

Eagles understand that the initial sale typically represents only a fraction of the potential opportunity within accounts. They know that as their accounts grow, change, merge, expand into new markets and even consolidate, that new applications, requirements, and opportunities will arise. They also realize that their customers are well-connected within their professional community and represent a deep source of referrals.

DO THE MATH

If you are not convinced that account reviews will generate enough new opportunities to keep your prospect pipeline full and justify the time and effort involved, just do the math. If you sold just one account per month for twelve months and then conducted an annual account review, this represents twelve possibilities in one year alone! In year two, this behavior will represent twenty-four possibilities, and so on. If you could identify and generate just 10 percent additional sales revenue from each account per year, that adds up to one new account per year! Additionally, if you acquired just one decent referral from each client—twelve per year—and successfully engaged with just 25 percent of those, that's another three new clients per year!

Most eagles figure this out early in their careers and invest substantial time and effort in account reviews. They view them as their personal marketing mission. Ask anyone who's been selling in the same field for twenty-plus years and steadily growing their business and they'll tell you that this is the golden key to longevity and maximum income potential.

FUTURE PACING ACCOUNT REVIEWS

The last item on your Implementation Agenda should be your first account review. This initial review may occur in the first ninety days, six months, or toward the end of the first year. Whatever your time frame, post the date on your Implementation Agenda and introduce your account-review process prior to closing the sale. The idea here is to position yourself as an ongoing consultative resource, not a hit-and-run salesperson.

Explain to your prospect what results you will be measuring. Now collaborate and engage the prospect by asking for additional suggestions as to what should be included. Together, decide on time frames, participants, and venues ahead of time, so that you both know what to expect.

Explain to your new client that account reviews are how you will validate your performance, and in turn, *earn the right* to ask for referrals. Simply tell new clients that you recognize them as being well-connected in their fields and that this is your way of leveraging your commitment to servicing and managing their accounts. Emphasize that this is the win/win outcome your strategic partnership provides both parties. Don't be surprised or jump at the chance if new clients offer you a referral or two right away. Be patient and insist on taking them up on their offers once you've *earned the right*.

VALIDATE THE VALUE

So what are the elements of an effective account review? First, you've cost-justified your proposal with measurable and sustainable outcomes — ROI, payback, cost reductions, increased productivity—so your account review should validate those outcomes.

Here's your opportunity—and your obligation—to formally prove that your product, service, and expertise is delivering the promised results. This is why it's critical to gather relative data during your discovery process; it provides a baseline for you to work from. You'll need to know the client's current productivity rates, sales revenues, operating costs, etc. prior to implementing your solutions, and then measure your effectiveness periodically to gauge the relative effects of those solutions and validate your value.

Many salespeople are at a disadvantage in protecting their accounts from competitive invasion because they don't effectively measure the results they deliver. This takes time and effort, but goes a long way toward justifying your value when contract-renewal time comes around, when your competitor gets in the back door or when your decision maker's superior wants them to shop around.

From a marketing perspective, look at the enormous potential for developing a repertoire of successful accounts as referrals. When approaching new prospects, you can point to these case studies to show the verifiable, sustainable, and tangible results you deliver.

Another element of an effective account review is a summary of how your solutions have helped your client meet the specific objectives that were identified in your consultative discovery process.

How have you helped your client overcome challenges? Has your solution helped implement corporate or departmental initiatives? The verification of these outcomes is critical if you are going to transcend the typical vendor status and position you and your organization as a trusted strategic partner on an ongoing basis.

TAKE THE PULSE

Another element of effective account reviews includes revisiting your consultative discovery process to determine if there are any new corporate or departmental initiatives, objectives, challenges, mandates, etc.

You should also identify any strategic changes that may present new applications for your products, services, and expertise. Get a good picture of the client's plans for growth, consolidation, or mergers. Understand any new technology or business processes that are being considered or currently implemented that may affect yours.

I guarantee you will be amazed at how much opportunity will fall in your path as a result of conducting ongoing discovery.

What's next? You've validated your value. You've identified new opportunities. Now, it's time to collaborate with your client to establish how you can add even more value and improve your service and relationship. Here are just a few questions to ask your client during account reviews:

- What are two or three things we're doing right?

- How can we improve?

- Do you have a vendor or strategic partner of the year award?

- What are the criteria for winning?

- What are your other strategic partners doing that you think is unique or powerful?

- How could we lose this account?

- What are your superiors thinking about us?

- What concerns do you have about the future in terms of our relationship or ability to fulfill our promises?

- Would you recommend us to your professional peers?

This last question is the perfect segue to the second reason you're conducting the account review — to gain referrals.

You've validated your value, collaborated on how you can help the client going forward, and learned how you can improve. At this point, if the account review has been a love fest, you've earned the right to ask for what you staged at the point of sale, and that is, a couple of referrals.

START THE CYCLE ALL OVER AGAIN

The process for gaining referrals is presented in Chapter 3 of this book. I suggest that you go back and revisit that process now that you have the complete picture on how to conduct account reviews.

Again, if you're tired of constantly jumping on the prospecting treadmill, burning out on your sales career, and asking yourself, "When does it get easier?" "How long can I keep doing this?" or "How can I multiply myself without hiring anyone?" master this process for win/win account reviews. Don't expect this to be less work than prospecting. It's not, but I guarantee that the results will be, by far, much more rewarding.

My Challenge to You

I believe that, at the end of the day, competitive distinction is up to you. It is not determined by more innovative products, better pricing, more marketing, or some temporary leg up on your competition. It is your competence, your implementation of a truly consultative sales process, and how you collaborate with prospects that will create the value prospects recognize and respond to positively.

In addition to the concepts presented in *PowerSelling*, there are some principles I must put forth that will be required from you in order to achieve extraordinary results — some things you must be willing to do on your own that will assure successful implementation of the ideas, methods, and tools provided in *PowerSelling*.

SIX PRINCIPLES FOR PERSONAL IMPLEMENTATION OF POWERSELLING

1. Misbehave

That's right. If you want competitive distinction, you must misbehave! For many of you, I know that's not a problem. What I mean is that in order to be distinctive, you must act distinctively. This means avoiding the temptation and trap of conforming to the behavior, sales processes, presentations, and proposals demonstrated by your competitors. You must also avoid conforming to the traditional expectations of your customers.

When I ask sales executives and salespeople why they do things the way they do, this is what I hear: "That's the way it's done in *our* industry," or, "That's the way we've always done it," or, even worse, "That's the way our customers want it," (or at least expect it). This is exactly the thinking that has conditioned your sales behavior and your customers' expectations. It results in a homogenized sales environment that makes creating competitive distinction close to impossible. Dare to be different. If you are willing to misbehave, you can create opportunities to innovate the way things are done in your industry and re-direct the customer's expectations with the outcome of leading the way, not following the competition.

2. Be a chooser

I learned this years ago from the top salesperson at MCI. When I asked him one secret to his success, he told me that he *chooses* which accounts in the marketplace he wants as customers. Once he chooses, he locks in on those targets, focusing his time and resources on them until he achieves his goal of landing them as accounts.

The principles of *PowerSelling* will not apply to every account. Some of the elements of this sales process will lengthen your sales cycle. Some prospects, especially price buyers, will not see the value of your consultative selling process. Some will see the value and still buy on price. Other accounts will be a perfect fit. It's up to you to identify those accounts that subscribe to value-based decision making and are willing to collaborate with you to design the best overall solution for their specific objectives.

3. Master tools

The sales eagles I work with use sales tools that prompt and support them in successful sales behavior, tools that help them stay focused, such as interview questions and proposal templates, for example. Tools that help them stay organized include prospect databases and time-management systems. Tools that help them present their business case convincingly include presentations with third-party white papers. Tools that help them track customer loyalty include customer-satisfaction surveys.

I know many salespeople like to look cool in front of prospects. They like to just show up and wing it. Most salespeople also loathe the "F" word — forms. But I notice that eagles don't worry about looking cool. They acquire, design, or shamelessly steal sales tools, and then master them much like a professional golfer masters each club in the bag. Like each club, there is an application for each tool and a related skill required to master each one. Eagles understand that mastering just a couple of tools, but not every one, could leave you in a sand trap with no way out.

4. Build skills

Lessons can be bought, but skills can not. Just taking a lesson — or reading this book — will yield very few results. If you want to master a skill, you must practice its application and *prepare to win*. Eagles are willing to go through the awkward phase of fumbling with new techniques. They practice skill-building until they are completely competent and confident.

If you decide to acquire a skill or sales tool presented in this book, please don't decide if it works or not until you have practiced the skill and are totally confident you can implement it with success. Next, don't decide if it works for you or if it doesn't until you have tried it at least ten times in the field. Like any newly acquired tool or skill, your first few attempts to use it will most likely leave plenty of room for adjustments and improvement. Try it, analyze your results, make minor adjustments, and try it again and again until it's yours.

5. Take risks

Above all, eagles have huge egos. They are uncomfortable in a comfort zone. They have a healthy self-esteem that allows them to take risks.

Some things in this book may sound a bit unconventional or even altogether crazy to you. Maybe there's a technique or tool that you don't think will apply to your industry or fit your personality. But what do you have to lose? You know the saying, "The greatest risk is not taking one." So what? You fall down. You get back up, dust yourself off, and try again. It's like learning to ride a bike when you were a kid. Did you get it the first time? Of course not. Did you worry about your comfort zone back then, even through all the bumps and scrapes? No. You were totally focused on the result—the freedom and adventure that the bike represented.

I urge you to shed the limitations of your comfort zone. Liberate yourself from the inhibitions created by your current success and be willing to get out of the box and try something new.

6. Get traction

Any instructor—whether they teach golf, piano, snowboarding, or science—will tell you that your retention level nose-dives as soon as you leave the classroom. Professional instructors are trained to break down the steps in the process they are teaching and instruct students to go out and practice each step immediately.

Pick three to five action items provided at the end of this conclusion and commit to embracing, customizing, practicing, and using them in conjunction with your existing sales process. Do something different tomorrow to create competitive distinction!

FINAL THOUGHT

I find that most people choose the unique and fortunate profession of selling based on the promises of creating unlimited income potential, endeavoring in challenging work, creating independence, and being fortunate enough to work *with people* instead of *working on things*. These are the precious rewards of the profession. I urge you to keep them in mind each day you practice your craft and to view each day as an opportunity to improve yourself.

My desire is not just for you to sell more, but for you to harness your personal potential to create the lifestyle that you desire, for you and those around you.

In this book, I have provided the impetus for salespeople to develop the attitudes, skills, knowledge, methods, and field tools that, when combined with your industry and product knowledge, people skills, persona, and personal motivation, hold the key to creating unlimited competitive distinction.

PowerSelling
Personal Implementation Checklist

Create Selling Opportunities at the Top

- Craft a marketing letter, telemarketing approach, and email message that address the seven questions prospects need answered before they say yes.

- Conduct your telemarketing to new prospects at either 7:30 in the morning or 5:30 in the afternoon.

- Start an objection log to capture the most common objections you encounter while prospecting.

- Categorize these objections as either needs, values, or fears, and then develop logical and compelling responses to each.

- Rehearse your responses until you are confident and competent in your delivery.

- Arrange a meeting with new prospects at either 7:30 in the morning or 5:30 in the afternoon.

Gaining Referrals

- On your next close, set a date for your first account review and tell your new client that you are going to earn the right to ask for two referrals at that time.

- Request reference letters from current clients that resemble the samples provided in Chapter 3.

- Attend a local networking event and scout out the eagles there. Develop a relationship with them and consider defecting from the original group to start your own group.

PowerSelling
Personal Implementation Checklist

Position Yourself as an Expert Resource

▪ Conduct a Pre-Call Investigation prior to your next sales call. Customize your opening conversation according to the information you obtain.

▪ Have a cup of coffee with your prospect—or some other kind of get-acquainted ritual—at the start of your next sales call.

▪ Craft your own Positioning Statement and practice your delivery until you can recite it brilliantly in forty seconds.

▪ Measure and quantify the results you deliver to your existing clients. Document and proclaim these results in your marketing message and sales presentation.

Conduct Consultative Discovery

▪ Craft a list of five to seven consultative discovery questions to appeal to and engage high-level decision makers.

▪ Craft a list of five to seven consultative discovery questions for mid-level decision makers.

▪ Craft a list of ground-level discovery questions for end-users and conduct a site survey.

▪ Format these questions onto a form. Use this prompter to record information on your next sales call.

PowerSelling
Personal Implementation Checklist

Propose and Present Your Value Proposition

- Craft an Executive Summary that fits your applications. Insert this step into your existing sales process prior to presenting your proposal.

- Create a winning proposal format that incorporates at least a Cost Analysis, Investment Justification, and an Implementation Agenda.

- List all the features, applications, and benefits your product or service program includes. Tailor your next demonstration or presentation to prove how these features fit the prospect's applications. Tie the feature to a benefit the prospect will gain by using the feature.

- Arrange your next client meeting at your facility and conduct an organizational tour.

- Try giving your prospect the price first!

Collaborate to Resolve Obstacles

- Start an objection log to capture the most common objections you encounter while trying to close the sale.

- Categorize the objections as either needs, values, or fears and then develop logical and compelling responses to each.

- Rehearse your responses until you are confident and competent in your delivery.

- Try a take-away close.

PowerSelling
Personal Implementation Checklist

Close the Sale and Expand Your Opportunity

- Pick two closing lines and commit to using them.

- Design an effective account review that will help you sell deeper and wider in the account and gain two referrals.

- Practice the six steps to implementation provided in the conclusion of *PowerSelling*.

POWER SELLING
CONSULT & COLLABORATE TO GAIN COMPETITIVE DISTINCTION

Order PowerSelling – "The Book"
@ www.powerselling.com
or by phone: (805) 650-1248

PowerSelling – "The Experience"

Inquire about *PowerSelling*–"The Experience," an intensive three-day course combining lecture, personal customization of field tools, role playing, and evening exercises which will equip participants to implement the proven principles, methods, and tools presented in Steven Power's book, *PowerSelling*.

Our learning experience goals include acquiring the attitudes, skills, and knowledge which will equip participants to perform at a higher level, learning from credible, real-world instructors, and leaving with turn-key field tools which prompt and support sales-people in implementing the *PowerSelling* process.

Put YOUR sales process on steroids!